STRONG
The truth about getting to the top
WOMAN

KARREN BRADY

STRONG

The truth about getting to the top

WOMAN

HARPER

For Sophia and Paolo.
Remember work turns dreams into reality.

This paperback edition published 2013

First published in 2012 by Collins
an imprint of HarperCollins*Publishers*
77–85 Fulham Palace Road,
London W6 8JB

www.harpercollins.co.uk

7 9 10 8 6

Copyright © Karren Brady 2012

Karren Brady asserts her moral right to
be identified as the author of this work

A catalogue record for this book is
available from the British Library

ISBN 978-0-00-741614-1

All photos provided by Karren Brady except: p.2 top and bottom right
© Mirrorpix; p.6 top © Roy Smiljanic; p.6 centre left © Ross Kinnaird/Getty Images
Sport/Getty Images; p.6 centre right © Action Images/Tony O'Brien;
p.7 bottom © Richard Lewis/Wire Images/Getty Images; p.8 top © Ian West/PA Wire; p.8
bottom left © Ken Mackay/Rex Features; p.8 bottom right
© Richard Young/Rex Features.

Printed and bound in Great Britain by
Clays Ltd, St Ives plc

CONTENTS

ACKNOWLEDGEMENTS

I've wanted to write this book for years and now that it's finished, I'm delighted as I really do think it can help make a positive difference for women all over the UK. So, thank you to all who have helped make this a reality for me – it's been an inspiring and productive journey and a large part of that has been down to working with a mostly female team!

So firstly I'd like to thank my Editor at Collins, Helena Nicholls, for working with me to arrive at a vision I'm proud of, and for her direction, professionalism and sense of humour! To the impressive Emma Rowley and Elizabeth Heathcote, thank you for all your wonderful work on the book. Georgina Atsiaris, Laura Lees and Tim Broughton at Collins – you're a creative and talented team. Thanks also to my agents Gordon Poole and Jonathan Shalit. To Lord Sugar and Martha Lane Fox, thank you so much for your generous endorsements. Finally to Paul, Sophia and Paolo, thank you for your love and support.

CH.1
MY MISSION

Canapés at Number 10 might not spark a eureka moment for every visitor, but they did for me. It was at a reception to mark International Women's Day at Downing Street that I realised I had to write this book. As a British businesswoman with a public profile, I am invited to many networking events and it must have been about the tenth year that I had gone along to this one. But what struck me this time – alarmed me, even – was that it was all the same faces yet again, year in, year out. Where was the new generation of women leaders, snapping at our heels? The new inventors? The new charity workers? The new scientists and lawyers? Where were the young women who were going to change the world? I was left with the distinct feeling that someone needed to inspire this generation of women, to get them going and help them through – hand on the baton, if you like.

My own career has seen me become, at the age of 23, the youngest managing director of a PLC in the UK, run two Premier League football clubs, sit on the boards of companies including Channel 4, Mothercare and Arcadia, and join the BBC show *The Apprentice*. Meanwhile I've got married, had two children and undergone brain surgery. Writing a book about my own experiences, I decided, telling things as they really have been for me, without glossing over any of the difficulties or pretending that it was easy, might help other women to think about developing their own road maps to success.

I want women to know they should never feel guilty about championing their own career while being a mother and should never – ever – be afraid to be ambitious. For women, that means considering the core values you need to succeed; visualising the place you want to work and the type of company and people you want to work for, or the type of business leader you want to be; then setting out to achieve this.

Ultimately, I want to change – fundamentally – the way people perceive working women. Even now, you know that if someone talks about *an ambitious man*, you immediately conjure up the image of a dynamic go-getter, someone you want to know, someone whose company you'd relish. Someone in control; a man going places; someone to admire. Yet exactly the opposite happens if you mention *an ambitious woman*. If they're honest, a lot of people immediately think, 'I bet she's a right hard-nosed bitch!'

I shouldn't have to spell this out, but I will: being an ambitious woman certainly doesn't mean you're a bitch. We have to change that thinking. In the same way, we have to change the perception of *feminism*. 'Feminism' has become a dirty word, so much so that, through stereotyping and media spin, few people like to be associated with anything to do with it. But a feminist is not someone who burns her bras and hates men. A feminist is simply someone who actively promotes the belief that women are equal to men. I hope, by the end of this book, you will embrace that belief and all that it means, too.

So, why am I so keen to see other women climb the ladder? It's simple. I love my career. I've combined it with being a mother, and I think I've been a success at both. That's why the description I think suits me best, more than chairperson, vice-chairperson or CEO, is working mother. That is what I am – a mother who works. My work and my children are the most important things in my life.

But there have been times when it has been very tough. I hope this book contains experiences and advice that will make the path easier for other women, and that it can offer some kind of inspiration when it's needed. It also signals my commitment to try to encourage, help and champion women from all different walks of life to achieve their potential. That's a promise.

I feel a personal responsibility in this, too. I have a teenage daughter, Sophia, who will soon take her first steps into a career. There have been a lot of changes for women at work in the 25 years since I was in Sophia's shoes – not all of them good – but changes still need to be made to support her and all young women.

Here's one of my pet hates. Companies will pay a lot of lip service to wanting more women to soar through the ranks, but they don't do anything about it. They'll say they're flexible when it comes to helping women combine work and home life, but when push comes to shove, it's a different story. A lot of businesses are only flexible when it suits them. But the best companies are those that are diverse. If you want different types of women, with different types of experiences and backgrounds, you just have to accept that they might have a family. You've got to provide the flexibility and support to allow them to succeed and, most importantly, understand that, although they may try, they can't be in two places at once.

Another niggle. When policymakers and the media talk about women in the workplace, we hear a lot about the 'glass ceiling'. Many people seem to think that every working woman wants to run a huge banking conglomerate and that if they don't they've somehow failed. But, actually, I've discovered that that isn't what most women in business want. They want a job they enjoy that pays enough for them to afford high-quality childcare and in which they are respected. Many women have a common aim: to fit a career around a family. Yes, we have to juggle and, yes, sometimes we have to leave work early because our family needs us, but that should not, and does not, affect our commitment and loyalty to our employers and our careers.

Why does this point need to be made, decades after women entered the modern workplace in their droves? Most business leaders are still male, and most male chief executives, chairmen or managers have a wife. And it's the wife who sorts out the school uniforms, who does the weekly supermarket shop, who gets the call from school when a child needs to go home sick, and all this allows the man a relatively stress-free path to the top. Good for them. The downside for their female employees is that when a woman says, 'My daughter's not well, I've got to go home,' there is little understanding. Women fear, with reason, they will meet a stony response, which makes them believe they can't combine a career with a family.

It's certainly far harder for women than for men to combine a career with children. Some of my male colleagues feel no compunction about going for a golfing weekend, or a boys' weekend, or a team-building weekend, or they don't bother to go and watch their son play football on a Saturday because they want a lie-in. Meanwhile I spend all my time at work or with my family. I could never say to my family, 'I'm going on a pampering weekend' – I just wouldn't feel comfortable thinking it, let alone saying it. The reality is that women who run companies are under far more scrutiny from their families about what they're doing when they're not with them than any of their male counterparts.

And in a way, this is understandable. In many cases women are more connected to their children than men are. But that does mean men don't tend to carry the same level of guilt. So women will want to be perfect mothers but perhaps they also want to run a business. And companies will increasingly have to accommodate that, because if they don't, women will leave and set up on their own: that way they can run the company the way they want to.

I do recognise that, in many ways, combining work and a family is easier for someone like me than it is for a woman who has a rigid nine-to-five job. I have reached the point in my career where I can be flexible. If there's a crisis at home and I need to be with my children, I can be – I'm the boss. But it wasn't always like that. I definitely didn't feel there was much flexibility when I had to go to work after three days' maternity leave. In fact, I was miserable.

That decision gets a mention in pretty much every newspaper profile of me, so I'm going to explain it once and for all. It was a mix of feeling scared, of not wanting to let anyone down, of feeling guilty for having had a baby in the first place and – if I'm being honest – not wanting this enormous change in my personal life to get in the way of the job I had to do. Most importantly, I was determined my employers wouldn't think I was incapable of carrying on as normal now that I had a baby. Looking back, all these years later, I still don't know how I did it! Up all night with a baby and at work all day. What I now appreciate, and didn't understand then, was that a career spans a lifetime, and that taking a few months off would not have harmed mine.

Nowadays, far more women are setting up businesses from their kitchen tables than ever before because they say to themselves: 'I won't work in a job that doesn't respect the fact that I have a family. I want both so I'll create my own flexible way of working.' And I'll be intrigued to see how many businesses are started by women rather than men over the next few years. It could become a big problem for businesses that will not accommodate women's needs.

The answer, I believe, is to have more women in the boardroom. The more women leaders we have, the better conditions will become for all working women. I don't believe in setting quotas, but I do believe that any public company that has no woman on the board should publish the reasons why. It would be sure to make very interesting reading. If a company came back and said, 'We have interviewed ten women and have not been able to find someone appropriate because the skills missing are this, this and this,' it would tell us a great deal about which skills we're not teaching young girls that they need to survive and thrive in a corporate world. Equally, if a company came back and admitted, 'We haven't interviewed any women for a position on our board,' that would be an embarrassing insight into the type of company it really was.

The suits in the boardrooms are not the only ones who have to change. It annoys me so much that the Government talks about getting more women into work, then doesn't help. Every woman who has to pay for childcare should be able to claim that cost as an allowance against tax: you can't work unless your kids are taken care of. It would make sense economically, too. Creating tax breaks for childcare would mean more revenue for the Government: at the moment, many mothers pay cash in hand for care. It would also mean that mothers could afford better childcare, which would allow them the peace of mind to focus on their work.

While I'm on my soapbox, another issue is particularly close to my heart: that young women should feel free to enter professions that have traditionally been seen as male. If my daughter wants to be a painter and decorator, a scientist or an engineer, I want that to seem like a perfectly natural choice. A generation of people still finds it weird that women would want a job in such an area. Those barriers need to come down. There should be a completely open path for young women to do whatever they want to do.

Too many young women pick up a magazine and see a host of glamorous models, with wardrobes full of handbags, married to footballers. They think that's what you have to aspire to, that such things give a woman value. Rubbish. When I meet young girls who tell me their ambition is to marry a footballer I always say, 'Why? Your ambition should be to own a football club!'

There can be nothing more soul-destroying than having a job you hate, even if you have never considered yourself a career woman. We need to encourage young women to open their minds to the possibilities of what they can achieve. Becoming an entrepreneur is nothing to do with your education. It's about your spirit. It's about your desire. A burning spark inside you that's your pride. If you have an idea, and the energy to see it into a business, you're an entrepreneur. I meet a lot of people with great ideas, but they lack the energy and determination to see them through. But if you're determined, with a steely core and a can-do attitude, you're an entrepreneur.

Sadly, since I started out, it's become vital to have a degree. My first job was with Saatchi & Saatchi, the legendary advertising agency. I joined them, aged 18, straight from school, and I don't think that could happen now. I don't think you'd get near a company like Saatchi's today without a degree, which is a great shame.

It seems to me that all companies are now looking for the same type of person – someone who has been to the right university and who has the right degree. That means there's little diversity within organisations, which can cause problems. You don't have people from different backgrounds with different experiences.

To me, it seems obvious that one of the problems behind the banking crisis was that the boardrooms were all full of people from similar backgrounds who followed each other off the edge of the cliff. Really good companies encourage their employees to question – 'Why aren't we doing this? What's going on here?' And that comes from having people who come from different backgrounds and look at things from different angles, to whom different issues are important. And, yes, that might mean not everyone has a 2:1 degree from Oxbridge or a redbrick university in their pocket.

I fear that talented people with great personal qualities won't get a chance. Not everyone wants to go to university, but many companies believe that if you have a university degree you're far more intelligent than someone who hasn't. That's not always the case. Life experience gives you the ability to think for yourself, the energy to provide for yourself and the desire to champion yourself.

Added to that, there's also a snobbery about which university you've been to. Young people could spend all that money and find that companies still turn their noses up at them because they've been to the wrong institution or chosen the wrong course. Despite all the talk about the glass ceiling, I think the biggest obstacle to entry into an organisation is the HR director. When you apply to a company now your CV goes into one of two piles – university, yes; non-university, no. And that definitely comes from HR.

But with the increased costs of university, so many people can't afford to go or are so fearful of debt that they won't go. And what happens to them? Either they have to be motivated enough to work for themselves, to come up with an idea and drive it forward, or they have to start at the absolute bottom and hope they'll find someone who notices their ability and is prepared to push them forward.

Companies will need to be more and more open-minded to unearth the right talent. At one point in my career I was offered a job as vice-president of a major IT company in Europe, which sounded great – on paper. Then they asked me to go to America for six months to complete an induction into their company. My response was, 'Why would you want to turn me into someone who has the same mind-set as everybody else who works for you? Surely it is better to have diversity.' But they were adamant: that was what they wanted. And, ultimately, it wasn't me.

On a more positive note, apprenticeships are a great way forward: you earn while you learn and you learn on the job. It's also an opportunity for the company, as the apprentices are with you from the outset and they become used to your way of doing things. Then, at the end of the process, they have a practical skill.

As well as looking past the letters – or lack of them – after your name, sexist stereotyping is another area that should be tackled to make sure the best women can rise to the top. We might think there is no sexism today, but there is. Strikingly, while I have rarely experienced it at work, I get it all the time from the media. If you look on Internet message boards, the abuse is always targeted at my gender: 'Oh, that Karren Brady, she can motivate the team – she knows how to put a spring in their step, nudge nudge.' They'd never say anything so personal about a male director, they would simply say he was really bad at his job.

Without a doubt, the hardest thing about being a female executive in the spotlight is that your gender makes you an easy target. Many women perhaps couldn't cope with some of the stuff I've had thrown at me, and I wouldn't blame them. Luckily, I have a very thick skin and I hope via this book to help you develop one, too. It can be achieved. You'll likely need it too, with the guilt the media encourages in working mothers. Newspapers will publish the research that fits their particular viewpoint – you know the headlines, they're the ones along the lines of 'Working mothers' children die young' or 'Working mothers' children are dyslexic/stupid/earn less money.' Either that, or it's stories about superwomen who have five children, a million-pound job and do it all perfectly – and, believe me, those stories are always misleading. Still, women measure themselves against them.

Then there's still this sense that if you have a career, children and a nanny, you're some sort of ruthless bitch who doesn't give a damn about anyone but yourself. That you just drop your kids off whenever it suits you and do as you like. That's hard for women to cope with. And it just is not true. Working women are weighed down with the guilt, either that they weren't at sports day or that they missed the board meeting. I want to help women to understand that you can only do what you can do. The balance is different for everyone.

What can I bring to this debate? Lessons born of hard-won experience. I am independent, driven and motivated. I have taught myself to rely on no one but myself. I don't pretend to be someone I'm not. I have self-esteem, and I know that I'm capable of achieving anything I put my mind to. Yet, as you'll read in this book, I never thought it would all turn out as it has. It's not been easy, and sometimes it's been punishing. But the result of 25 years' hard work is that I'm fortunate: I have a career I love.

And that comes with a warning. I did not wake up at the age of 42 and parachute into this position. I've worked hard, sacrificed a lot, and all the time I've been in pursuit of success. Yet I can say, with my hand on my heart, that it's been worth it. That's why I hope to inspire you not to feel guilty for having a dream, for having ambition and not being afraid to go out there to do something about it. To turn your dream into reality.

After all, if you don't champion your career, who will do it for you?

I want to make things better for my daughter, for you and yours.

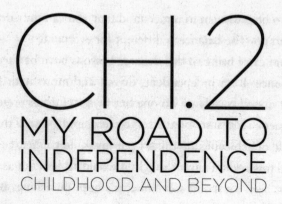

CH.2
MY ROAD TO
INDEPENDENCE
CHILDHOOD AND BEYOND

Ambitious, driven, determined – that's how people talk about me, I know, and I guess I they're right. But to me these words are empty because they say nothing about what really counts, what pushes a person forward. For me, the one thing more than anything else that's motivated me, the goal I have been striving to reach all my life, is independence. More than money, fame or glamour, I have always been driven by that desire: to live a life where no one could ever tell me what to do. One where only I would have control over me and no one could tell me what to think or how to act.

I've always been this way. I still am. I shudder at the thought of ever having to ask anyone for money to buy a new coat or a lipstick. And it's this drive, more than any other, which has got me out of bed every day, has made me push myself forward to success.

So where did the desire for independence, the need for control or, well, sheer bloody-mindedness come from? Writing this book, I've had to dwell on how and – a much harder question to answer – why I became who I am. I don't reflect on such things easily, because I've never been an emotional person. That's an understatement, if ever there was one: I'm logic personified! It's not quite 'Call me Spock' but I'm the sort of person who, when a door shuts, never opens it again. I march forward and never glance back to the path behind me. It's helped me throughout my career: I don't waste time second-guessing my decisions and pondering the what-ifs. And up until now, I've never really questioned why I'm like this. Yet looking back over my life, as I tried to work out how and where the desire for independence began to make itself felt, I realised I could pinpoint it exactly.

I was three years old when my mum and nan left me at home one day with my grandfather, while they went shopping. I remember my parents had this elegant drinks cabinet in the lounge. As a toddler, I was fascinated by it. The door folded down and all these beautiful little glasses and different-coloured bottles glinted away in the backlight. I decided to get a chair, climb up and have a good look. Everything looked even better close up. The dainty little glasses (for sherry), the perfect size for me, were so tempting that I started to fill them up with the green, yellow and clear liquids I saw in the bottles: crème de menthe, advocaat and vodka, I know now! Taking little sips and inviting my dolls to do the same, I was having a wonderful time – until my grandfather came into the room and asked what I was doing. Of course, as soon as he twigged, he told me to stop. Three-year-old me instantly replied, 'This is my house and I'll do as I want.' He left me to it. He was married to my grandmother, so perhaps he knew not to pick a losing fight!

Unsurprisingly, when my mum and nan got home I was rolling drunk and, by all accounts, not much more co-operative. My grandfather got an earful, I was put to bed, and the story passed into family lore for ever more. As my nan used to tell me: 'You were such a little cow – and you know what? You weren't sick, not once. Not a drop.' When you've got that streak in you as a toddler, no one's ever going to be able to tell you what to do when you're fully grown.

It wasn't a one-off, either. A few months later my mum took me to school for the very first time. Picking me up after my first day, she asked the teacher how I had got on. She'd been worried, my mum admitted, as I was very shy. 'Which one is your daughter?' the teacher asked.

'Karren Brady,' said my mother.

'Karren Brady?' was the incredulous response. 'Shy? She walked in, pulled a boy off his chair and said, "That's my seat. Move." I wouldn't be worried if I was you!' It was advice my mother took to heart. In fact, that was probably the last time she worried about me.

Not that this mind-set always made things easy. I went to boarding school when I was thirteen, and that was tough in many ways, but the hardest thing of all was the lack of freedom or choice. You had to write on a noticeboard when you wanted a bath, booking a slot! Then you had twenty minutes to wash out a bath someone else had just used, bathe, dry and get dressed. It was always a rush, and it's probably why even now I can't sit in a bathtub for longer than a few minutes without thinking I should get out, get on, get moving. Another thing I hated was having nothing of my own. Not my own bed, not my own pillows, not even a drawer that belonged to me. I was stuck in a dormitory with lots of other girls. Some snored. Some talked all night. Some I couldn't stand.

I remember realising while I was there that if I wanted to ensure I was never – in emotional terms – put in a place like that again, to ensure that nobody would ever be able to say to me, 'I am in control of you and you will do what I say, you will eat what I say, you will bathe when I say, you will wear what I say,' I had to be independent. And, for that, it was clear, I would need funds. It didn't worry me that I had no dreams that matched the desire for money. There was no job I wanted, no career I felt drawn to. I would have happily worked on a market stall if I'd thought it would make me money. That said, I wasn't then and I'm not now driven by money, but I knew it was the means to independence and that drove me forward.

Boarding school makes my early life sound all ponies and privilege, but before I went I'd had a very normal upbringing. I lived with my mum and dad, Rita and Terry, and my brother, Darren, my elder by 18 months, in Edmonton, north London. Until I was 13, I went to a number of different schools, including the local comprehensive. My father was a businessman, in printing, and – whatever that word signals – ambitious. He was starting to make his way in the world, and as he hit his milestones, our life changed, quite visibly. So during my childhood we went from living in a very small terraced house in Mitchell Road which backed on to the milk depot to a slightly bigger three-bedroom house in Empire Avenue, then into a much bigger detached house on the Ridgeway, Cuffley. By the time I was 17, we had an estate in Crews Hill.

That meant there was a powerful feeling all around me, all the way through my childhood, that you could achieve most things through hard work. My father worked all the time and gradually it started to pay off. My mum got a sports car, my dad a Rolls-Royce, we started to go on fancy holidays, my brother and I were eventually moved to private schools – and it was all the result of hard graft. If my dad pulled off a big deal, he would take us to a posh children's clothes shop in Golders Green called Please Mum and fit us out, which was always exciting. There was never any feeling that he was doing this for himself: his hard work was for the whole family.

It was never just about wanting more. The way I see it, if you have a bit of a spirit in you, you don't want it broken. That means you can end up finding within yourself a relentless energy and a capacity for hard work to realise your ambitions. In this country, we tend to think that ambition and ruthlessness come hand in hand – that if you're ambitious, you're not a very nice person – but I don't think that's true at all. I think ambitious people are just the ones who have an inner pride. A spark that sets them apart. They don't just accept their lot. They're fighters and grafters and they claw their way out of often difficult circumstances. Alan Sugar is like that, and so is my father. Dad came from very humble origins, not knowing who his father was and with a mother who had to work very hard all her life.

In fact, my dad definitely has all the attributes of an achiever. A lot of people fear failure so much that they can't achieve anything. They may have the great ideas but they can't turn them into reality. But my father does. He's a real go-getter. He understands that saying yes is always the way to do it. He's a 'Yes-yes-yes-until-it's-no' man. He understands that you have to be personable, able to make decisions and relentlessly hard-working in order to achieve.

As for my mum, she was a conventional mother and house-wife and had a different sort of influence on me. She was very glamorous – she and my dad would go out every Saturday night, and every week she had a new dress, with her cigarettes dyed to match the colour of her outfit. She's still amazed at my achievements and some of the things I do. That said, she has her own steely side and can hold her own in any situation.

Still, the atmosphere I grew up in was not the sort where you set yourself goals and went off and delivered them. It was more a leave-no-stone-unturned, keep-trying, keep-grafting philosophy. We were always striving to do better and that has been a very important influence on me. I don't just look at where things are and think, This is OK. I look at how things could be better. Good, I find, is always a barrier to being great. If things are good, you don't want to rock the boat. And some people, some businesses, can't see why you'd want to change anything about good. But to be great you have to forsake good and take risks. In business, a lot of people settle for the way things are. They don't have that vision of how things could be improved, or understand that by sheer hard work and gritting your teeth you can make them better. That was a lesson I learnt from my dad and it was a good one.

It may sound contradictory, but although my father's example of hard work was so important to me, he didn't really push me or expect a great deal from me, and probably at some points in my life I didn't expect much of myself either. I wasn't naturally gifted at anything. I wasn't keen on sports, I wasn't the best at art, I wasn't academic – I wasn't the best at anything. In fact I was a very average child who really didn't know what she was going to do or where she was going to go.

I remember feeling ill every time I got a school report, as I'd inevitably get some mediocre grade that would result in a 'Brady bollocking' because my parents thought I didn't try hard enough. I don't remember being particularly bothered about those, unpleasant as they were, but I do think they helped me gain an underlying steely drive. I was determined to show my parents that when it really mattered I would come into my own. I wasn't sure when that would be, or how I would achieve it, but I knew somehow I would do something – something better than they expected me to do anyway.

It was that stubborn streak coming out, as it always did. When my brother was 17 my dad bought him a Ferrari as his first car. Not a lot of parents would give their teenage son a car like that, I know, but as I've said, my dad loved sharing his success with his family. I had a Ford, but I soon gave it up, got a loan and bought a battered old Golf. Even then I knew it was better to have a battered old car and my freedom.

I do think that, subconsciously, I wanted my parents to be proud of me. I have heard that they are a million times by now but, of course, it doesn't mean as much when we're older. Yet even when I was young, I could easily have cut myself away from my family. And I did for a while, going off to do my own thing, without the need for their approval or disapproval. It came back to that independence of mine – I didn't want anything from them and I didn't want them to want anything from me.

I'm close to my parents today, though. I speak to my dad every day and I see him and Mum at least once a week. They love my children, and my dad comes to watch the football regularly. He's supported my husband Paul in his football career, too, first as a player, now as a manager. I know they're there for me, no matter what.

Of course there were other powerful influences in my childhood. Both of my grandmothers were hard workers, strong women and very important in moulding me. I was very close to my mother's mother in particular, who put end to that alcoholic tea party when I was three. Grandma Nina was dynamite. She was Italian, from Naples, and incredibly feisty. She would have killed for her family – she wouldn't have thought twice about it. If someone cut up my grandfather in traffic, she would get out of the car and punch them on the nose.

I'm sure it won't come as any surprise when I say that she was definitely the one in control of her house and marriage. Grandma Nina would say when, she would say how, she would say how many. She was great with money – not because she had a lot, but she knew the price of everything and she was in charge. My grandfather, Gerald, went out to work as a postman, but she would take his wages and give him cash to spend. That was just the way it was. My brother and I would often spend weekends and holidays with them and she was in and out of our house, so we spent a lot of time together.

Grandma Nina really believed in me. Her attitude was: you can do it, so go out there and get on with it. She always pushed me forward: 'Get to the front of the queue!' She was very competitive on my and Darren's behalf and she was an amazing role model. I looked up to her and loved her very much. And if I get a bit feisty at home my husband will still say to me, 'Oh, Nina's here. Nina's coming out.'

My father's mother, Grandma Rose, was another hard worker. She worked till she was nearly 80 in the Corkscrew, a famous London wine bar, where she baked the pies and cooked the meals. Another very independent woman. I miss them both a lot, now that they are no longer with us.

All these strong characters in my family tree passed something on to me, I am sure. From an early age I was a self-sufficient child, happy with my own company – which I still am. I don't think anyone can teach you that: it's the way you're born. I'd be in my room all the time, watching my telly, and my parents would call up, 'Are you going to come down?' but I would refuse. I wasn't unhappy – I just liked to do my own thing.

And I liked things my way and wanted to make my own decisions. I remember once being on holiday with my parents when I was 10 and they decided we should all have a sleep in the afternoon. Of course, I had different ideas. Darren, who would have been 11, and I sat in the lounge of the self-catering apartment we had and made up a song called 'Half A Beer Saint

Allier' after finding a bottle of it in the fridge. We'd sing, 'Half a beer Saint Allier round and round,' and spin the bottle. When the bottle stopped, it was time to take a swig. Needless to say, we were roaring drunk when our parents woke up. They blamed me, even though Darren was older. They were probably right to do so. To this day I've never been able to drink beer without remembering that afternoon!

Speaking my mind was always my only option. In situations where other people would keep their mouths shut for a quiet life, I was the opposite. Darren used to say to me, 'Why do you have to say what everyone else is thinking? Why do you do that?' But biting my tongue just wasn't me – if I had something to say I wanted to be able to say it, which caused some eye-rolling. 'Oh, Karren!'

I was fiercely determined. If I wanted something and my parents wouldn't give it to me, I'd find a way to get it for myself. I was never given pocket money: my parents always said, 'If you need something, let us know,' which was very kind of them, but I wanted to be in charge of my own money. I recall them once saying no to something I wanted, I can't remember what it was – but I haven't forgotten what I decided to do. I put up signs in my bedroom window – it was my bedroom so I could do what I liked, I reasoned – saying, 'Massages, manicures, come inside!' My mother was shouting up, 'Who are all these weirdoes coming to the door?' and I bawled back, 'They're my customers!'

I was definitely bloody-minded. I once put up a Vote Labour poster in my bedroom just because my parents were Conservatives. 'Take that down!' my dad roared.

'It's my bedroom!'

He said, 'What does the poster even mean?' and I didn't know, of course, I just knew it would wind him up and cause a debate.

I wasn't all trouble, though. From an early age I had enormous energy and an appetite for hard work. I used to get up at five o'clock in the morning and go to work with Nanny Nina, who was an office cleaner. No one made me do that – I enjoyed it. Even then I just really liked working. And to this day I love cleaning.

Another thing I learnt when I was very young was never to take no as the final answer, that there is always room for a bit more manoeuvring. At my boarding school you were given a limited number of weekend passes to go home. I quickly worked out that if you asked all the time and the nuns felt they were always saying no, they were more likely to say yes – eventually. So I'd ask every weekend. They'd say no, so I'd say, 'Well, you've said no five times and it's important,' and they'd give in. In the end, I had more time at home than anybody else, through strategy and sheer persistence.

Despite all the effort I made to go home, I was confident that I could take care of myself. My mother used to say, 'You're absolutely fearless, I don't know where you get it from.' Even as a young child I wanted to go out on my own, do my own thing. I longed to be independent. Before I was boarding, I took the bus to school from an early age, and on Saturdays I'd go to Wood Green, not far from where we lived, which had a high street and a bit of bustle. I think eventually my parents just thought, Oh, get on with it – I was a bit too much for them.

When I was about 14, I'd tell my mum I was going to stay the night with my best friend, Charlotte, who would tell her mum she was staying at my house. Then we would meet up with our clothes in carrier bags, get changed, take the Tube into central London and go out in Soho. When everything closed we'd walk around until the Tube restarted in the early morning and go back to our borough, Enfield, walk around until 10, then go home. Mum would say, 'Well, you look very tired.' But she never knew.

Years later, when I told her, she was shocked, but I was even more shocked by what she said to me. She looked at my daughter and said, 'What goes around, come around.' I went very cold and felt terrible about what I had done. But at the time I couldn't have cared less. Nothing was going to happen to me: I was in control, I was safe – or, at least, I thought I was. But if I imagine my 15-year-old going out all night now, well …

But back then I was at that point when you're not a child but not quite an adult. I thought I knew everything and I would voice my opinions all the time. If someone said black, I'd say white, just because.

Once, my father invited me to some do with a lot of businesspeople. I'd heard him say that one of them had gone bankrupt twice and had 'knocked' a lot of people, then set up in business again. I didn't quite know what that meant but I knew it wasn't very good. Dad was talking to this man, who made a negative comment about someone I knew.

'How can you say that when you go round knocking people?' I asked. Everyone stared at the floor and my dad tried to laugh it off. I continued, 'But it's true, though, isn't it? How can you criticise somebody when that's the way you do things?' I think Dad secretly liked it, because I was saying what everyone was thinking. Mind you, it was the first and last event like that he ever took me to!

I wasn't naughty or spiteful or vindictive, but I was quite demanding, opinionated and defiant. I like to think I was free-spirited, but my parents obviously didn't agree! All in all, I must have been quite a nerve-racking daughter, and maybe that's partly why my parents sent me to the nuns – they couldn't rein me in.

My school, Poles Convent, was in the middle of nowhere, in Hertfordshire. The school doesn't exist any more – the building is now a golf club and very beautiful.

People will say, 'This is your school?'

And I say, 'It really wasn't like this then.'

It was an unhappy place, a bit like something out of Dickens. There was a long drive up to the school with two cattle grids and you knew when you'd gone over the second that you were past the point of no return; it was just awful. My closest friend, my-all-night-in-Soho companion, who went there too, says that her lasting memory of the school is that she was always unhappy and hungry, which just about sums it up.

It was very religious, with mass twice a day. Everyone was bored and restless, and it wasn't as though you were even getting a really good education, because the teaching was variable. And you had no life experiences, because you never met anybody. It was very isolating and I was a bit of a loner. I didn't have many friends because I didn't want many friends. There were a lot of geeky, closeted girls who'd never seen anything, never been anywhere, never done anything, for whom going into Ware town centre nearby was the most amazing thing you could imagine. I just found the things they were into mind-numbingly boring. They thought it was great to stay up all night reading *Jackie* magazine, or watch Wimbledon all day.

Still, some of the girls did things that I would never have dreamed of doing. I was feisty and spirited but I wouldn't smuggle boys or booze into the bedroom. There were lines I didn't cross and that was as much about my father's wrath as anything. My parents were easy-going to a point, but if you crossed that point ... I would get as close to the barrier as I could and push against it, but I knew when to stop.

In those days my father had interests in the music business and I would take my friends to pop concerts. We'd have back-stage passes to everything from Live Aid to Paul Young, which created a bit of jealousy at school, where the atmosphere was very emotional – girls got worked up about trivial things, unable to take a mature view. You can imagine, with all those teenage girls cooped up with too little to do, things would get out of proportion. But I'm not that sort of person. I don't get emotional – if something goes wrong I try to solve the problem.

The only time I really enjoyed Poles was when I could throw myself into a project like a school play, when I'd put myself up as the director. It wasn't that I wanted to be off drinking or doing things I shouldn't, it was just that I couldn't do what I wanted, whatever that happened to be.

What Poles Convent School did give me, however, was resilience and a belief in God that didn't come from the hundreds of masses I attended, but from another experience. My friends and I were late back to school one afternoon, so I decided we'd tell the nuns that I'd hurt my ankle and we'd had to walk back very slowly. I was a good actress and laid on the pain very thick. So much so that the nuns decided to take me to hospital for an X-ray. I braced myself for a row, but at the hospital, after they'd done the X-ray, the staff told me my ankle was broken. I ended up spending that whole Easter in a cast. I realised that God moves in mysterious ways!

Divine intervention couldn't get me out of that school though. I knew I had to spend years there and that all I could do was endure it. Even now I do things I don't want to do because they need to be done. School taught me to stick things out.

Poles didn't have a sixth form – thankfully! – so when I was 16 my parents had a rethink. Even they could see that Poles had left me without any life experience, and they looked for something a bit different. They sent me to Aldenham School in Elstree, a boys' school that had been founded by a brewer some 500 years ago and took girls in the sixth form. It was quite a transition: from being surrounded by girls I went somewhere where I'd be spending all my time with boys.

I had some of the best times of my life at Aldenham and, looking back, I would say that was where my confidence began to build, with the sense that I could be whatever I wanted to be. Aldenham was a much more mature school than the convent, which suited me. You were given a lot of independence. You were expected to behave responsibly, so you did. In that respect, it was the opposite of Poles. At Aldenham I went from having no real experiences, never knowing any freedom, straight into this university-style school that had its own pub, allowed you to go out, and provided an environment for personalities to develop and adapt.

It's interesting that two other successful businesswomen, Martha Lane Fox and Nicola Horlick, went to boys' schools. All my friends at Aldenham were boys, and after Poles, it was a breath of fresh air. It suited me to be in a less emotional atmosphere. There was none of the jealousy there had been in my old school. Things were just simpler.

I made friends with four boys who were a year above me and we were like the musketeers – we did everything together, went everywhere together. People thought it was strange that we were a group of one girl and four boys, but those men are still my friends today – they were at my wedding, my children's christenings and they come to my house to visit.

Living alongside them taught me a lot about where boys are coming from, and it's pretty basic stuff. I think girls are like cats – we like our independence, want you only when we want you and like to be left alone sometimes. When we want something we'll come to you, but most of the time we don't want anything. Boys are like dogs – they need lots of exercise, lots of food and lots of pats on the head. To me, they're simple creatures, very easy to work out. None of them tried to dominate me, something you might worry about if you pitched a girl into a school full of teenage boys. Mostly they seemed to want to look after me, but I didn't need looking after. They all had their own little problems that I helped them with. I never really had any problems because I was quite happy with my life. And if I did have a problem, I never felt the need to discuss it.

So Aldenham taught me to hold my own, and it also provided a real insight into how to conduct myself around men. I learnt when not to be one of the lads. There was a real culture among some of the girls of matching the boys pint for pint, and that wasn't me at all.

Still, much as I preferred Aldenham to the convent, I had a difficult year when my four friends left. I didn't know anyone in my own year very well and so spent twelve months waiting for time to pass and school to finish. Another lesson in endurance: grit your teeth and get on with it.

I did the minimum amount of work for my A levels, but I used my initiative to help me through. In history, three subjects always came up, so of course I learnt those thoroughly. However, when I picked up the exam paper, there were questions only on two, leaving me a subject short. I had absolutely nothing to fall back on. But one of the other questions was, 'Does a good history book make a good novel?' I invented a book about the Second World War called *My Struggle* to fit the bill and wrote reams about it. I knew a little bit of German, so threw a few words in. Then the examination board wrote to the school asking for a copy of the book. There was a hairy moment when my housemaster asked me, 'Does this book exist?' and I insisted, 'Of course it does!' In the end, I said it was at my grandmother's ... and ended up with a B! If I've got to find my way around something, I will. I'm very resourceful.

And I do think boarding school, despite the frustrations and restrictions, was the making of me. It taught me to keep pushing the boundaries and showed me my strengths and what I was good at. I might not have been academic, but the challenges helped me realise I had valuable qualities: pride, a relentless drive, the capacity to make the best of difficult situations and self-reliance.

I left school at 18, having decided that I didn't want to go to university. University was and is a great place to become a professional – a dentist, a lawyer, a doctor – but not necessarily for someone interested in marketing or sales, which was more my line. I wanted to go straight to work and start making money. To get on that road to independence.

I'd already had Saturday jobs, even though I'd been turned down for the first job I'd applied for, at Waitrose in Enfield. I'd gone in wearing a typical 16-year-old's get-up with a pair of high-heeled white cowboy boots, and the guy said, 'You can't work here! You're far too glamorous. You wouldn't like it.'

'No, I really want to. I need the money and I want to earn,' I said, but he wouldn't employ me. I have never set foot inside a Waitrose store since that day.

Instead I'd got a job in a hairdresser's, working on the reception desk. By the end of the first day I had completely reorganised it. I'd reworked the rotas, changed the opening hours, reset the till and redone the pricing. I was even advising people on what they should have done with their hair. I think the staff were a bit shocked – 'You can't do that, you don't know anything about hair' – but I said, 'Well, you can tell red hair's not going to suit that person.' To me it was just logic; there was no real art to realising that someone should go dark instead of blonde. And once they got used to me they appreciated me and were sorry when the holidays ended and I had to go back to school.

By this point, Dad was saying to me, 'What are we going to do with you? What job are you going to get?' He had a friend who worked at an estate agent's, so it was sorted: 'You can be an estate agent.' Logical, like me. I did go for the interview but then I thought, What am I doing here? I don't want to be an estate agent. So I refused to take it any further. That great drive for independence was tied to a determination that no one was going to tell me what to eat for breakfast, let alone what to do with my life.

Fortunately, Aldenham had laid on lots of careers days where different companies came in and talked to us, including Saatchi & Saatchi, and LBC, the London radio station. Lots of people were interested, but whereas everybody else thought maybe they'd write to them at some point, I made sure I had all the right details before the people left and the next day I was on the phone making appointments to see them. I wasn't going to leave things to chance.

And both companies I was interested in offered me a job. I chose Saatchi's, leaving school on the Friday and starting work there the following Monday. Even though I was only 18, Saatchi's put me on their graduate programme – I guess they saw something in me. I don't think that would happen today, which is a shame.

The '80s was a really interesting time to work at an advertising agency and I loved it. It always amazed me how people moaned about their jobs. I loved getting up and going to work, and Saatchi's was a really free and creative environment. There was no mould – you didn't have to be a certain person from a certain place.

From the start I wanted to take on more responsibility. I arrived early and was the last to leave. To be honest, I was never really sure if that was just because I loved it or because I had nowhere else to be. I was living in a house without central heating or a washing machine, so I was certainly in no rush to get home! What also surprised me was that some of the people I worked with spent all day thinking about what they were going to do after work. I wanted to be first in, last out and to volunteer for everything. I'd put my hand up whenever they asked for someone to do something – even if I didn't know what they were asking for I'd say, 'I'll do it.' That gave me a real edge.

I also wanted to be in the know. I wanted to meet the right people so I'd get noticed. Every Christmas, Saatchi's had a big party and I would work out who I wanted to meet – the chairman or whoever it was – and go up to them. 'I'm so pleased you're here,' I'd say, 'because I really wanted to tell you about such and such,' or 'I really wanted to discuss this with you.' I understood then something I tell a lot of women who work for me now: nobody will champion you or your career if you don't.

I never waited for someone to say, 'You did a good job.' I'd be saying to people, 'Look at what I've done! Isn't it great? Shouldn't I head up the next project?' To me, that was a more straightforward approach.

But even though I loved Saatchi's the graduate programme was very rigid – you had to do this for six months, then that for six months, and I started to feel impatient. I think the turning point came while I was working on the Boursin cheese account. One of my jobs was to go into supermarkets and see where it was displayed, talk to the manager about why it wasn't more prominent and file a report. Then I would go back the next week, do the same and see, over several weeks, how it was moved.

To me, that seemed the wrong way of doing things. I assumed that the prime position must be at eye level in the middle of the shelf. But when I went in on the first week all the Boursin was tucked away at the bottom where people couldn't see it. So I simply moved it to the middle section, with its price label, and I'd go back every week and check it was still in the middle. But Saatchi's were furious with me: that task was what the client paid them for.

I decided to move on, but with the intention of going back to Saatchi's later. I thought if I went elsewhere and got some more experience I could reapply to Saatchi's and miss out a year of the boring structured training. I was in such a hurry. I don't know if that was ambition – I've never really understood why

I was racing – but I wanted to get ahead as quickly as possible. I wanted that independence and security.

So I went from advertising and Saatchi's to LBC, and from there to work for David Sullivan, at Sport Newspapers. Three different companies, and three different industries. In my eyes, that's no bad thing. I meet very few women who knew at a young age what they wanted to do. Most of us find something we're good at, then have a look around and think, You know what? I'm the best person in the room doing this so I should be running this team of people, I should be running this floor, I should be running this office, I should be running this business. Success is about making the best of your skills, whatever they are. If it's your personality or your ability to put your back into something, make the best of it.

For me it was definitely a slow realisation of ability. I didn't have a dying ambition to work in advertising or radio or football. I didn't mind what it was as long as I could do it. I just wanted to find a job where I could be the best.

There is a certain story that often comes up in articles about me, when, as a 19-year-old selling radio advertising space, I pitched to David Sullivan. I had been given *Asian Hour* to sell, which was pretty tough – a four–five a.m. slot, the real grave-yard shift. I had been handed a list of companies that spent money on advertising but who didn't advertise on radio, and one was Sport Newspapers.

I got through to David Sullivan on the phone, and he said he wasn't interested, that radio didn't work. I decided I would drop off some material at his office – persistence is everything – and once I was there I decided to wait and meet him in person. I waited and waited and waited, and in the end he agreed to see me because I had waited so long. I did a very quick pitch to him and he wasn't buying it at all, so I said, 'Look, if you take the advertising and sales don't go up, you don't have to pay for it.'

He said, 'That sounds good to me.'

I didn't have the authority to do a deal like that, so it was a risk, but I remember thinking, Well, if it doesn't work out, what's the worst that can happen? They can fire me but I can always get another job – I'm only 19. I still use that kind of thinking and I have done all my life. In fact, it's the foundation of my confidence and my ability to take risks. That episode is often considered to have been a turning point in my professional life, but in truth I think my life had been heading that way since I was a young child.

And it worked out. Sales at Sport Newspapers went up and within months Sullivan was spending more than £2 million a year on radio advertising. I was managing it all and earning more commission than all the other sales staff put together. And then he offered me a job, which I accepted. People tend to jump to conclusions about the pornography associations of Sport Newspapers, but I wasn't working on any top-shelf titles. I was working on the *Sunday Sport*, and the paper was very different in those days. Nonetheless I still get criticism about that time – people say, 'How can you stand up for women's rights when you worked in the porn business?' Well, the answer is that I didn't work in the porn business. To me, that criticism is a bit like saying, 'Sky has an adult channel, so if you work for Sky that means you work in pornography.' Of course it doesn't.

I realise that all this might make getting started sound easy, but there were costs – even if I thought they were worth paying. One small example: at Saatchi's I always dressed the part. Everyone else would turn up in jeans and a T-shirt, and there would be me, immaculate in a suit. That meant that if a client came in I would always be the one selected to go and meet them, introduce them and take them round. This was a way to stand out. It would have been far more comfortable to sit in a pair of jeans and a T-shirt, but that was not the person I wanted to be.

When I was a child and Dad had made a bit of money but I was still at the local comprehensive, he would pick me up from school in his Rolls-Royce. That was difficult for me because when you're a kid you want to fit in. It made me a target. I'd say, 'Dad!' but he'd say, 'What's the problem? You should be proud.' I remember thinking then that there was nothing worse than always being on the outside, and the urge to fit in is strong – but I guess that, ultimately, my ambition was stronger.

I had to weigh it up. When we left school my friends were off on gap years, travelling the world, or they were at university, or working in pubs while they relaxed for a while. Meanwhile I was in the office at seven a.m., and never had the energy for anything else. I didn't get drunk after work or go clubbing at weekends. I remember David Sullivan saying to me, 'It's half past ten. Why are you still in the office? You're 20 years old.'

'Well, it's really important, and if I don't get it done, who's going to do it?'

'It can wait till tomorrow. You've got to have a life as well.'

But that wasn't what I wanted. I remember that a good friend and her boyfriend were temporarily stuck for somewhere to stay, so they came to live with me in my London flat in the Docklands. She said to me, 'Karren, you've never used this kitchen. There's no kettle, no knife, no fork. I've opened the dishwasher and the brochure's still inside. The oven's still sealed up. You don't have a life. Do you realise you don't have a life? You eat at your desk morning, lunch and evening.'

But I didn't care. I was doing what I wanted to do. The thought of going to a nightclub terrified me then and it terrifies me now. It's just not me. I wanted to work and I loved work.

So that was what I did.

CH.3
MY MIND-SET

So at 18 I was on my way. Yet to some people it might have seemed that I had scuppered my chances at the very first hurdle. It had been crystal clear at my interview at Saatchi & Saatchi that I was not quite as creative as the world's top advertising agency might want their staff to be.

At one point I was shown a picture of a cornfield and asked what I saw. 'A cornfield?' was my blunt reply. Then they showed me a picture of a cornfield in blue, and asked me again what I saw. 'A blue cornfield.' When they showed me the same picture in red, I knew what they were expecting – some arty-farty inter-pretation, which I could have waffled on about – but instead I said the opposite: 'This is a red cornfield.'

And while I can see how you might explain this to a client as something deep and meaningful, which communicates their brand in an imaginative way, I think it's important that the staff at any organisation are allowed to see things logically and are not afraid to call things as they see them – internally, at least. We're not all Picassos, and that's fine.

As it was, the creative director interviewing me laughed and asked me a final question: 'If you had to choose between an Yves Saint Laurent coat and a Marks & Spencer's coat, which would you choose?'

Well, I pondered, and replied: 'It depends on who's paying.'

That was on the Friday and I started work on the Monday. What I drew from that was that my interviewers had understood I was different, that I had spoken up for myself, and that I would stand out. I was not creative – I can't even draw a stick man – but I had something else to offer: I was professional, direct and mature. Far more mature than any other 18-year-old they had met. And I had left a lasting impression, which was ultimately more useful to me than being able to talk convincingly about the meaning of some blue corn. Just as well, because that was not me.

Yes, I was a teenager, but they saw that I wanted to go places. I had incredible energy and strength of character, which came from my confidence, and I wasn't afraid of anything. That meant that when I started work I threw myself into every aspect of life at the company.

And I was happy to do so. It amazes me that people spend tens of thousands of pounds on working hard at university but when they're being paid tens of thousands of pounds by an employer they begrudge the hard work and dedication it takes to get what you want.

On one occasion, someone asked me if I played tennis, as one of the Mr Saatchis was having a tournament at his house and someone on the team had gone sick. I was county level, I said, when the truth, of course, was that I was the least sporty person I knew. I went anyway and established myself with the people who mattered. I grasped every opportunity to get my face known in that organisation, matching my ambition with an outward presence. It gave them confidence in me, and my age was irrelevant.

Making sure I looked the part, spoke the part, read every piece of material about the company, understood what every department within it did, meant that, while I was not creative in an artistic sense, I could communicate, give opinions and talk about any aspect of the company. I read about our clients, understood their businesses and made myself a valuable and indispensable member of a team. I was loyal and dedicated to the company. People knew from my attitude that I would never let them down, even at 18. There were plenty of people at Saatchi's with degrees in business, art, design and technology. But I had things they did not have: personality, drive and a relentless energy.

That's why I know that the person you are and your mind-set are at least as important as qualifications or background in relation to how successful you will be. Other than O and A levels, I don't have any qualifications. Instead I put my success down to certain qualities. Some I was born with, some are a product of different influences, and some I have had to work to develop. Another person will have different strengths and different skills that they can develop.

That said, certain traits have been invaluable to me in my working life. I've said it before and I'll say it again: confidence is always key. I have never let people put me down, make me feel inferior or say that I wasn't good at something. It's about being able to say, 'I'm sorry, you may think that's acceptable behaviour, but I don't.' I think that comes from that inner belief in myself – I have a very a strong core. To a certain extent I believe I was born with that, and I realise others will not feel the same, but it also came from a good basic education and the independence that boarding school gave me. It was there that I really learnt to rely on myself. Others will face different challenges in which they can begin to develop that self-reliance.

Tied to confidence, for me, is the ability to stand up for myself and to say what I think. I have never been particularly worried about offending people. When I was younger, people used to say to me, 'Sometimes it's easier to keep your mouth shut and get on with it,' but I didn't want to because I knew that then I'd lie in bed all night, thinking, I wish I'd said something. Other people might not be quite so outspoken – and it would be a boring world if we were all the same – but I do think that in life you regret what you didn't do far more than what you did. You'll always kick yourself for not saying what you thought at certain times and it can play on your mind for years. It's not just the quick reply you wish you'd made – though of course that can be deeply satisfying! – it's about making your mark, standing up for what you believe.

Even I have not always done this, and one occasion still rankles with me. I was in a meeting with the representative of a shopping centre where West Ham United had a shop with a two-year lease that could not be broken. I had been brought into the club as vice-chairman after David Sullivan and David Gold, who owns the high-street chain Ann Summers, took control in 2010.

My team was trying to do a deal to extend the lease for a much longer term but on a reduced rent – an offer that meant all parties had to compromise. But the person on the other side was so disgracefully rude to me and my staff that at one point I pushed the chair back, ready to get up and storm out.

Yet I didn't walk away as, at the time, I didn't think it would resolve anything. Looking back, nothing was resolved anyway, so I bitterly regret not telling the bloke to shove it. On the other hand, I've walked out on football deals, thrown agents out of my office, put my foot down and, ultimately, got what I wanted. There's no need to be rude but sometimes plain speaking is the only answer. Of course, it's easier to say what you think when it feels like there's less on the line. That's why I find that the deals in which you're less tied to a certain outcome are the best deals you do – you tend to push harder. And there's a lesson in that.

The twin sister of confidence is self-esteem. Self-esteem eliminates fear. There are a lot of people who would love to do something but they're too frightened it won't work, or that if it does work, they won't be able to cope with it. I am one of those people who always says yes, and then works out how it all fits in. I think I get that attitude directly from my father.

Yet self-esteem is an issue for many women, and I honestly don't know why. I don't know if it's about education – whether there isn't enough emphasis in schools on girls taking risks and pushing themselves forward. I've always had to make up for my lack of intellect with my drive, my work ethic and my personality. I think that if you do really well at school, you grow up believing things will come to you naturally because they always have. Then when you get out into the world and you're not automatically the best at everything, and things don't always go your way, it's much more difficult to cope. If you're always in the bottom half of the table, and you have ambition, you have to develop other skills to compensate.

I should add that what I see as self-esteem is predominantly about valuing yourself and your opinions, and not being afraid to voice them. When I was much younger, the ways in which I expressed – and developed – my self-esteem was by dressing well and sitting in the front row at any company meeting. When I spoke up, I ensured that I made a valuable and interesting contribution, which is vastly different from talking for the sake of it. I learnt never to belittle my contributions, and to say thank you when people paid me a compliment about my work. I didn't say, 'It's nothing,' because it wasn't nothing. And if I didn't value it, who would?

Never confuse self-esteem with being cocky, though. A know-all is worse than a know-nothing. But if you have knowledge of a subject you can voice an opinion confidently and make people start listening. You'll start to form your reputation within an organisation. Being well-read, considered in your approach and making points that are worth listening to means that others will value your input. And understanding who you are and what you want out of life will help you discover the stepping stones to gaining the assurance you need. A confident person can say with ease, 'I'm sorry, but what exactly are you asking me to do?' when they are unclear about it. They won't be afraid to ask and feel confused or worried.

My road map to understanding who I was and what I wanted to become started when I began to wonder, when I was at school, about the sort of company I wanted to work for; the sort of people I wanted to work with. Other people will find different paths to discovering these things, but that doesn't matter – as long as you do.

So those are the fundamental elements of my mind-set. But how does it translate in the real world, and into dealing with other people on a day-to-day basis? With me, in the words of

Lord Sugar, what you see is what you get. I am very straight-forward. I'm one of the very few people I know who has been married for sixteen years, and I've still got the same friends I had when I was at school. I don't get it right all the time, but I think those things are an achievement. They come down to the fact that my friends, family and the people around me know who I am, and I never feel the need to pretend to be anything else. Too often I see people present themselves as one person when actually they're another, and at some point it always becomes clear that their life is built on quicksand.

There is never anything wishy-washy about my instructions: I'm always straight-talking and direct. Everyone who works for me knows exactly what I expect from them, exactly what their contribution is to the company and how they fit into the over-all structure. This is both an asset and a coping mechanism, because I do so many things. I don't have time to pretty things up. I can do it if I have to – if I'm the spokesperson for a particular issue, it may be part of the job – but the ability to do many things has always been at the heart of my work. There are simply not enough hours in the day to sit down, have a coffee and be sugary.

Instead I get people in and say, 'Right, this is what we need to do, this is how I think we need to do it, this is your role, your contribution to the plan, and if the company is successful and you do your bit, this is how you will be rewarded.' I take all emotion out of it and find I work well with others who share that philosophy. Lord Sugar operates in a very similar fashion. We would both say, however, that taking the emotion out of it doesn't mean you have to be cold or unfeeling. It's about being clear, precise and operationally succinct. Everyone should know in which direction they are going, who is doing what and why.

It is not about being a bully and it is most certainly not about stopping people's progress. It is never 'my way or the highway'. But it is about being able to make decisions and communicate them clearly. I was taught never to look down on people unless I was helping them up and I believe in this whole-heartedly. I also believe that you cannot judge anyone's ability – for a promotion, for example – unless you have told them the judging criteria. If they know what you want, if they are clear on what they have to do, then they can get on and achieve. Working as a team should never be about guesswork.

Similarly, I have never needed flattery or sycophantic approval, and that may be because I never got it when I was young or perhaps because I care only about what those closest to me think: my family, my staff, my team. I know I'm good at what I do so I don't care what people on the outside think. You can spend your whole life worrying about what people are saying about you, but you have no control over that. And the best way to deal with it is to develop a thick skin.

I am not a sensitive person, but my skin became even thicker when I first went to Birmingham City as managing director, after David Sullivan bought the club. Back then, the press thought I was a publicity stunt when I showed up in 1993 at the age of 23 to run a football club. As a woman, my looks and the way I dressed came under a lot of scrutiny. I couldn't understand it – it wasn't as though I was there to manage a team or play football: I had gone to run a business.

All that attention might have been a distraction. I couldn't let that happen – I didn't have time – so I decided that the only thing that mattered to me was that my chairman and bosses were pleased with what I was doing. If I was going to be used as a distraction, I would use it to help promote my business. If I had to appear in a football kit to make sure the sponsor paid a fortune and the picture made the front page, so be it. But I did it with a purpose and I didn't let myself be bothered by what the man down the road thought – and that's how I think today. I'm confident in the work I'm doing, I'm confident my board is happy, and that's all that matters.

Another thing that I really believe has been key to my own success is personality – a bit of presence, or charm, you might call it. I can walk up to people to talk, and make an impression that stays with them. It helps if you enjoy that kind of thing, of course, but if you don't, it's that old philosophy of mine: what's to lose?

When I was first working for David Sullivan, he was doing a lot of business with Northern and Shell, the big publishing company owned by Richard Desmond. There was some problem that was proving hard to resolve, so the 19-year-old me offered to go over and talk to Richard and see if we could sort it out. I think David had tried everything, and he knew I was dogged and determined, so he said yes.

Within a couple of hours Richard and I had sorted out a deal that everybody was happy with. An issue that had been threatening two organisations was resolved. He offered me a job on the spot. 'You've so impressed me I want you to come and work for me,' he said.

I said, 'OK. You've got to pay me 38 grand a year and you've got to give me a car.' Remember, this was 1987, so that was a lot of money, never mind for a teenager. He wouldn't pay it. I never heard back from him.

Then, 20 years later, when he had taken over the Express newspapers, he rang and invited me to lunch. When we met he told me, 'I've followed your career. I've seen you rise.' Then he said, 'Something that you can never have known is that the night you asked me for 38 grand I went out to dinner with a group of bankers and I said to them, "I've spent the day with the most impressive teenager I've ever met, but she wants 38 grand a year, and it would really upset the applecart in my company to give a 19-year-old that much money."'

Apparently the bankers said, 'Well, if she's that good give her the money,' but Richard had decided that it would make things too difficult in the ranks.

'That is such a huge regret of mine,' he told me, those two decades later. He had been thinking about it for years, he said, and told me he wasn't surprised to see that I had on gone to be a success – and that he was now ready to pay me 38 grand a year! Obviously, my price had gone up a bit since then, never mind inflation. We laughed about it, and I call him a friend.

After all, he's a character similar to me. He will follow his ambitions wherever it takes him. He will take on established organisations, with established methods, and change them. He also knows that to change something and change it for the better are two very different things. Richard changes things for the better and is able to establish both a creative energy and a strong business sense across his organisations. To be able to encourage excellence and integrity is a rare talent. Incidentally, Saatchi's stood for those qualities in the '80s and that was why it was one of the most fantastic places on the planet to work.

So, I know that I have the sort of personality that can open doors with certain types of people. And, again, it's about playing to your strengths and using your skills in the best way possible. I suspect that in a more corporate, grey-suited environment I would scare people to death: I'd never toe the company line if I didn't believe in it. And I do like to be in charge of setting the strategy, the company ethos, what we believe in and how we demonstrate it to ourselves and our customers. I could not imagine working in a place where there was no expectation, no room to progress, no respect for who I was and what I could contribute.

Where possible, I believe in promotion from within. I like to mentor and guide my staff to be the best they can be, spotting talent and enhancing it. Most people have talent, but it's hidden behind self-doubt. Nothing gives me greater pleasure than to help someone become the best they can be, to help them fulfil their work ambitions and have confidence in the quality of what they produce. People from different backgrounds, with different experiences, coming together with one objective, one aim: that's what excites me, that's what makes me tick nowadays.

And, to achieve that, you need to have faith in yourself. In 2010 I was awarded an honorary doctorate in business from the University of Birmingham and, when I received it, I gave a talk to the graduates. I said to them, 'No matter how much you know, you have to have the personality to deliver it. People need to have confidence in what you're saying, and you have to have the confidence to convey that.'

I'd go a bit further – to be successful, you also have to have balls. You need that bit of aggression to get the job done and lead well. I've always been pretty tough, whether that's about being able to stand up for myself, or to be straight-talking, and I believe that comes back to always wanting to win: I've always pushed the boundaries to get what I want. Ultimately, I credit my nan Nina, who was certainly a woman with balls. She was never scared to stick up for herself or to push me forward. My mother says I'm fearless, and maybe that's true. I certainly don't like letting anyone get one over on me, which may sound a bit less heroic but can mean the same thing!

Here's an example. When I first started work, I was mugged. I was living in Enfield, and as I pulled up in my car one evening a man walked out of my front door. 'Can I help you?' I asked.

He said, 'I'm with the police. You've been burgled.' But when I asked to see his ID, he pushed me to the ground, snatched my handbag and drove off. I drove after him – I didn't even think about it. I'd just bought myself, for the first time, shoes and a matching handbag, and he had taken the handbag. He could have had anything else but not that!

I ended up cornering him in a cul-de-sac, where I jumped out of my car, ran up to him and tried to get the keys out of his car so that he couldn't go anywhere. I was fishing around in the back of his car looking for my handbag and I was so angry I hit him over the head with a flask I found on the seat, yelling, 'Give me the handbag – keep the contents, just give me the handbag!'

Then he pulled out a knife, and I said, 'Okay, fine, go.'

I called the police, and they didn't do anything, but I'd made a note of the number plate of the man's car and drove around Enfield until I found it, abandoned. I think I got the handbag back, but I can't remember now. What I do remember is that the story made the local paper with a real '80s headline: 'Have-a-go Yuppie'.

And I do know I'm at my absolute best when the chips are down. That's an operational style, and I think you only really know what yours is when you're under real pressure. It's how you manage people, what you do, how you cope, what you say, how you go about challenging someone.

That's why your approach to problems is very important. If you panic in the face of a problem, you're going to have an unhappy life because life is a series of problems. How happy you are relates to the solutions you find to deal with them. I don't panic. In fact, I love problems and challenges.

For me, a problem is an opportunity to show off my talent and put everything I know into action; this is an attitude that has underpinned my whole career. I understand that the way to deal with a problem is to break it down, work out what the elements are, then start to fix them. If I think back to the day that I first met David Sullivan, when I sat outside his office and pitched the deal to him to buy airtime on LBC, that situation came out of a problem. I had no clients, I had no money coming in and I had to go and fix it.

Often the solution requires hard work, of course. It is ingrained in my DNA that nothing can substitute for the sheer hours you put in. I saw hard work all around me as I was growing up – if you want to be successful, you have to graft – and that gave me great energy.

I also learned that you shouldn't be ashamed to try anything. If I had a cleaning job I wouldn't be ashamed – I'd just make sure I was the best cleaner. When I say to my husband, 'Darling, I could live in a caravan with you and be happy,' he says, 'Yes, but knowing you, if we lived in a caravan, you'd work until we got the best caravan with the best view.' And I know that's true. I'll always work hard to improve my situation: I'm ambitious.

I want to be the best and I'm ambitious, but I've never seen that as requiring me to be nasty. I think that comes back again to my inner core: a belief that I can win. I'd pitch myself against anybody at the things I know I'm good at. But I don't need to be unpleasant to people to be successful because, if I'm tested, I believe I can match others and win.

It's never about being nasty. I hate bullies – I know how it feels to be on the outside – and there are far better ways to get the best out of people than by bullying them. It's much better to encourage them: that way you give them confidence. It's the same with children. If you say to a child, 'You're naughty and you're no good at anything,' they will be naughty because they think that is what they have to be. If you say to them, 'You're great, you're good, you're really talented,' then they feel they're someone with things to give. Of course, every now and then when you're running a business, you've got to give people the push they need, but you don't need to be a bitch.

Instead, I aim to instil loyalty in my staff. Loyalty is very important to me. I am a very loyal person, I have very loyal friends, and you can't put a price on that. It's the most important ingredient in running a business. The best thing I do is work with people I admire, who are talented and successful, and I know so many things about so many different people that

I would never talk about. I have never been a gossip, and that is one of the reasons why I work for Simon Cowell's company and Sir Philip Green's board, and have worked with David Sullivan for more than 20 years. It is about loyalty and understanding the position you're in.

When the chips are down you need to know you have loyal people around you. I sometimes ask myself who, in my organisation, if I rang them up at three o'clock in the morning and said, 'I need you now, there's a crisis,' would embrace the challenge and look forward to being part of the solution, and who wouldn't answer the phone. Confidence under pressure comes from the belief deep down that you are not on your own. I have had David Sullivan in my life for virtually the whole of my career, and I know, if things get tough, that he will be on my side. Loyalty goes both ways.

And loyalty is created by mutual respect, by promoting people and allowing them to take credit for their work, and standing in front of them when things have not gone right. 'Protect and serve' is the motto of the LA police, but it's also true of good leaders and how they deal with their staff and customers. My staff know that I will deal with them directly. I will promote them and protect them. I will never hide behind any of them, but I'll always let them hide behind me.

Now, everyone who knows me would say I'm fiercely competitive. I am not competitive about sport, or personal possessions, fame or money, but when it comes to business I'm one of the most competitive people I know. I could never see the point in running around a track to be the fastest. But when my skill set is being assessed, I have to admit that I want to be the best. When I was team leader on *The Apprentice* for Comic Relief, I had to win. My focus was entirely on that – not on being on TV, not on getting the glory jobs: it was about leading my team to victory. I am competitive about the things I think are really important, the things I stand for.

But I do think you can be too competitive. When I was younger I wanted to win everything, and I would get fiercely passionate about the tiniest challenge. I was very feisty – always fighting my corner. I remember David Sullivan saying to me, 'Don't try to win everything. Just win the things that are important.' It was very good advice. It led to an understanding that not every detail can be controlled at all times – even though I'd like it to be!

My attitude also changed when I became the team leader, as opposed to the team player. You spend all your young life being the team player who wants to be the team leader, and once you get there you realise what it actually means to lead. You can't be this hugely competitive individual any more, protecting your own glory. You have to bring out the best in everyone else.

Plus, I'm in my forties now and, like everybody, I've changed and matured over the years. It's hard to believe, but I have mellowed – a bit! I have definitely become more tolerant – you learn that when you have children, since as a parent you have to develop patience. When I was younger I had far less tolerance, which meant I ended up doing everything myself.

In fact, delegating terrified the life out of me. I had to have control and I wouldn't let anyone else in. It wasn't that I didn't trust people; I just didn't think anyone could do it as well as I could. Like lots of young people, I thought I knew everything. It's only as you get older that you realise it's far more important to learn than to teach.

So I have learnt how to teach people my values, how to develop a vision and have faith to let my team help me deliver it. And I have been very lucky in that people tend to work for me for a long, long time, so they know my level and what I'm looking for. They enjoy the structure and the freedom, which is an unusual combination but – as I have found – a winning one.

CH.4
ENTERING A MAN'S WORLD

Of course, no man – or woman – is an island and you don't operate in isolation throughout your career. However much you have perfected your mind-set, you have to navigate and grow within your working world. For most of my life, that has been football.

People are amazed when I say this, but I'm no great fan of the game. When we – David Sullivan, David Gold and I – bought Birmingham City Football Club in 1993, I wasn't thinking, 'Oh, I love, love, love football, I have to get into it.' But there were many things about the business that interested me. And that was why David Sullivan and I made a perfect combination. He loved the football, and I loved the business.

Because football is a unique business. We don't manufacture anything at all. Instead, it's about making the most of the brand and getting the best out of the people. And all your assets are people. Dealing with them correctly, getting the balance right between them, understanding who they are and their ambitions, setting a structure for success and making sure everybody is going in the same direction are the keys to running that sort of people business.

What I liked most was the connection with the customer, the ability to build a brand, which, in turn, builds value. There are very few businesses that have such a real, intimate relationship with their customers, and still fewer that come face to face with those hard-core customers every week. And football is unique in that the customer almost never changes his allegiance. It's not as if an Aston Villa fan ever wakes up one morning and decides to support Birmingham, or an Arsenal supporter is strolling down the road and switches to Tottenham. When you're in, you're in, and I thought that was a really interesting concept. I wanted to explore just how far you could take the relationship.

And I do love brands. I love the idea of building loyalty and building the concept, and I could see the potential with a football club. When I got involved all those years ago, no one would have said a football club was a brand. At the start, there were lots of people who said they supported a club but who weren't paying customers. They would sit at home, watch a match on TV and say, 'I support Birmingham,' but they wouldn't express that support by buying a ticket, a programme, a shirt. I saw great potential in those people. I was convinced we could find a way to convert the passive supporter into a paying customer who would engage in the business of football.

I was right. Now it has all changed: everyone accepts that the crest means something special. In fact, by the time I left Birmingham you could have a Birmingham City credit card, a Birmingham City mobile phone and you could travel with the Birmingham City travel club. We even had a Birmingham City funeral service (which one or two of my managers were threatened with over the years!). My point is that over the years the brand had been recognised and extended. People believed in the company, and they believed in the directors, so we were able to extend that loyalty – and so, the brand – into other non-football-related businesses. I saw that opportunity in 1993 and I was part of that change, which was massively gratifying to see.

It's not that you have to totally love every aspect of a business you are involved in, but you do have to have a passion for it. You have to understand the business: what it needs and how to run it. Of course, to some extent, all businesses are the same – simply put, you have money coming in and money going out, and you just have to make sure that the first sum is bigger than the second.

And I would say, in that respect, not being a big fan has been an advantage throughout my career in football. Where most people go wrong in football stems from their support for the club: it becomes the overwhelming consideration when making a decision. They overspend because they think that the team reflects personally on themselves. They say yes to everything because they're so desperate for the club to be a success on the pitch. They forget that it's important, too, to be a success off it. They are a supporter first and a businessperson second. That can be a dangerous trap.

When I first came into football, David Dein, a true gentleman and a friend, who was vice-chairman of Arsenal at the time, gave me a great piece of advice. He said, 'Never let your heart rule your head in football – and never believe the manager when he says, "Just one more player."' That has been proved true to me over and over again. Although I admit that during Birmingham City's Barry Fry days, when the squad swelled to 50 players, David might have wondered if I'd forgotten his advice!

Over the years I have found that most of my male counterparts are just frustrated managers. They don't really want to be the chief exec mopping up all the day-to-day boring, complicated and less glamorous issues: they want to be on the training pitch, buying and selling the players, and in the changing room – and, secretly, they all think they're good enough to do it.

I can't think of anything I'd want less. Some of my managers say to me, 'Will you come to the training ground?' I say, 'What for?' At West Ham, I've been to the training ground once. In 16 years at Birmingham City I probably went 10 times. If I thought I could do a better job than the manager, then we'd all be in trouble. And if my managers realised why I'd turned up at the training ground, they might stop asking! If I'm there it's always bad news for the manager – he's probably about to lose his job.

Nonetheless, football didn't find me, I found football. It all began when I saw a small ad in the *Financial Times*, saying 'Football Club For Sale'. By then, I had been working for David Sullivan at Sport Newspapers for three years. My main responsibility was as sales and marketing director – I orchestrated the marketing campaigns, ran the sales team and controlled costs – but no one at Sports Newspapers really had one job. I had soon grasped that when you work for a small business you have to be everything: the financial director, the marketing director, the sales manager. You do the selling, and you make the tea, too. It was hard work and great fun. When I was there, the *Sunday Sport* had a circulation of more than a million copies and was the equivalent of the US *National Enquirer*. 'World War II Bomber Found On Moon' and 'Hitler Was A Woman' were our typical sort of headlines. We spent a few years, under David's shrewd and inspirational guidance, building a fun company into a £50 million empire.

Still, I didn't have one single clear idea of where I was going or what I wanted to do next. There was no grand plan. I was enjoying my job, enjoying being hands on and taking on more responsibility, and I was loyal to my board. After all, they had made me a director at the age of 19 to keep me motivated, giving me kudos which probably didn't exist outside my own head! I loved it, and if they had said, 'Karren, you're going to Australia to run a pig farm now,' I would have said, 'Fine, I'll give it a go.'

Now, at the time, I knew David wanted to get into sport. He was thinking about horse racing and I was thinking about football. We had looked at a few clubs – some were too small, such as Barnet, and some were too big, such as Spurs – and then I saw the ad for Birmingham City, which was in administration and, as I'd discover, just right.

I went to visit the club on a Friday, came back and told David that the place was a mess but that we should buy it. Having seen it, I was hungry for the challenge, something new and exciting. It took the weekend to persuade him. I was on the phone to him every 10 minutes, saying, 'You do want this, you do, you do. Whatever money you put in, I'll get back.' He was 60 per cent against it, more inclined to say no than yes. But I was 100 per cent for it.

He told me he just wasn't sure, that he was worried football clubs were a black hole for money – which, in the main, they were and still are – but I told him I'd go up there and do everything that was necessary to make a success of it. And, in the end, he backed me. David took a really big chance on me, giving me Birmingham to run when I was still just 23, and I will always be grateful to him for that.

So, by the Monday, I was managing director of a football club. David had seen what was coming, and warned me,

'Football is a very male-dominated business, and you are going to have to be twice as good as the men to be considered even half as good.' I just replied, 'Luckily, that's not difficult!' And that was how I felt. I had no idea that anyone would be interested in a female managing director – after all, I wasn't going to manage the team.

I knew I'd come up against some outdated beliefs, so there were no real surprises there, but what was a shock, as I've said, was the level of press interest. I think it was due to the heady combination of my being young and a powerful, modern, independent woman who'd had the cheek and balls to come and run a football club. At the time I really couldn't work out what all the fuss was about, but the media were fascinated by this young woman getting involved in football and I had to deal with that.

I remember Kelvin Mackenzie, then the *Sun* editor, calling me in my first week in charge and asking me to do an exclusive photo shoot with his paper. 'Why on earth would I want to do that?' I asked, and he explained how it worked. I did the photo shoot, got coverage for the football club, which helped to build its profile, and both parties were happy. Kelvin taught me the importance of *being* the promotion in true Richard Branson style. This was the start of my relationship with the *Sun*, where I have been a proud columnist for the past six years. It's *my* paper, loyal to me from the start, and as I've said, loyalty is very important to me. I've been asked to join the *Daily Mail*, the

News of the World, the *Guardian*, but I have never been able to break the real loyalty I felt for the *Sun*. I even went on to work with Kelvin as a consultant when he started TalkSport, helping him with its start-up, devising shows and coming up with ideas. An editor and a businessman – what a combination. Shame he's a Charlton fan!

When I gave my first press conference at Birmingham, I was desperate to look older than I was so I put on my big earrings and my wide shoulder pads and did my hair up. My aim was to look 25 because that seemed so much older than 23, at that age. I went on to the stage to outline what we intended to do for the club, and at the end I asked for questions. Of course, that was when a journalist from the *Sunday People* put his hand up and said 'What are your vital statistics, love?' For a minute, I thought, This is going to be a mountain to climb, but I told him, 'Listen, I know I am not a man, I know it's difficult for you, this young woman coming into football, but I promise you, in 10 years' time, you'll find us playing in the best league in the world, and setting the standard other football clubs will follow.' Then I flicked my big hair and walked off stage. As I passed him, he said, 'You may not have a dick but you have got great big balls.'

He was right, I don't have a dick! But I do have big balls and I needed them. If you're a woman in a male world, you need to put a marker down early and say, 'I'm tough. I'll lead the company by having integrity and professionalism. I will stand up for what I want, I will make improvements and I will deliver solutions.' In the end, I found that the business was easier than the players.

When my first manager, Terry Cooper, invited me to travel with the team to an away game at Newcastle, I immediately said yes, thinking it was a lovely offer. Let me tell you, spending all those hours on a bus with 35 men and one small toilet is why I have never set foot on the team bus again. Then, as I walked back to my seat after one of my doomed toilet visits, one of the players said to me, 'I can see your tits from here.'

'Well, when I sell you to Crewe, you won't be able to see them from there,' I replied. And I did sell him, too. Strangely, that was the last bit of lip I ever had from any player. Barry Fry, our manager at Birmingham City, said in his biography that at first he'd thought I'd be a bimbo but that he'd come to see me as a hard bastard, and maybe that was true for a lot of them. And, funnily enough, when Barry bought Peterborough he was on the phone to me, crying and moaning about difficult managers who couldn't understand the meaning of the word 'no' and begging me to help him sort the mess out. He had learnt just how difficult it was to be in charge of all aspects of a football club. I did laugh at the irony of it, but I helped him because I liked him.

It wasn't just the players, of course. There were some absolutely prehistoric attitudes throughout the industry. On our first away game at Watford, I arrived and asked for the boardroom – the place where the directors meet for lunch and a drink before the game. But the steward on the door kept trying to send me to the area reserved for directors' wives, called the ladies' room. 'Actually, I'm the managing director of Birmingham City,' I ended up saying.

He peered at me and said, 'Oh, yes, you're *that* woman. Stay here and I'll find out what to do with you.' Then he had to ring someone because, unbelievably, even in 1993 the football boardrooms were still men only. Women were banned and sent off to the ladies' rooms. I never went to a ladies' room myself, but I'm sure that anything that happened there was far more interesting than anything that ever took place in a boardroom. But, of course, that wasn't the point. With me coming along and making a fuss, ladies' rooms were closed and women were finally allowed to go into the boardrooms. I had made my first major breakthrough, and had had my first chance to change things for women in the game.

Yet from within the business itself, from my colleagues, I would say that I really didn't experience any sexism at all. In fact, it was quite the opposite: I had a lot of support, a lot of help, a lot of advice. It comes back to that unique thing about football: the fans don't change their allegiance. That means football is a business in which there is almost no competition. People in football understand that, and also that the more football clubs work together, the better it is for us all. Obviously, it is not quite as simple as that – there's rivalry among us on a match day – but in the main, everyone is very pleasant to me.

And sometimes I found friends in unexpected places. I'd spend all day running the business and attend every event involving the club in the evening. I'd visit schools and potential sponsors, getting to know the movers and shakers both in the industry and in Birmingham, a city I had never even been to before the Friday I'd gone to visit the club. It was at one of those evening parties in Birmingham that I met my counterpart at our rivals Aston Villa. Doug Ellis was known as Deadly Doug for his tough, unrelenting attitude towards pretty much anyone he met. He eyed me up and down, walked over and asked me where I was from. Obviously not an avid reader of the *Sun*! 'I'm from Birmingham,' I replied.

'Ah, the council?' he said.

'No – the football club!' We laughed. That was the start of a great friendship. People thought that, as the clubs were rivals, the boards should be too. But nothing could have been further from the truth. Doug has been a great friend and very support- ive; he has my respect.

But the most important thing for me to do back then was not to make friends, it was to make an impression – and quickly. I had arrived in a wave of unexpected publicity, all blonde hair and short skirts, as the press kept pointing out. I knew I had a mountain to climb in terms of being taken seriously. But I had a job to do, a career to carve out and a promise to keep to

David Sullivan – that I'd protect his investment. I was not, in any way, shape or form, going to be deterred from that aim. I worked 16 hours a day, every day. David had bought the club and put me in charge of running it after we had had three successful years together at Sport Newspapers. It was a big decision and I wasn't going to let him down. So I changed things quickly to show my understanding of the business. Also, I wanted to make an impact.

Birmingham City was in administration when I took over and heading for oblivion. I had to strip the business right down and instil a different mentality. That meant the first thing I did was sack almost everybody. David once described me as a 'sacker'. That's about me being someone who can deal with confrontation, while lots of people – even very senior, success-ful people – don't like it, can't do it and avoid it at all costs. I can get on and do it; I have to think of the bigger picture. A company is only as good as its staff, and if the staff are poor, the company is poor. Sometimes as the leader you have no choice: if you want to survive, you have to be prepared to make changes for the betterment of the company. And if you look at companies that go into administration – as Birmingham had – it is usually because they're overstaffed. They're unfocused and not streamlined enough.

I take no pleasure in firing people – only a psychopath would enjoy it – but those people at Birmingham could not have delivered my plans. The business was not just run down in terms of the facilities, it was run down in turns of the customers and the staff who worked there. The staff had no idea where the club was going, let alone how to get there. There was no leader, no understanding that this was a business. The club's chief scout, out there searching for talent, was also the catering manager!

What those days taught me is that if you have to fire someone you must do it yourself. I had inherited a secretary, and she was such a lovely woman but she could only manage one badly typed heavily Tippexed letter a day. She would come in and say, 'I'm sorry to bother you,' and then it would take her five minutes to explain what she wanted. In those five minutes I could have done another ten things. It was very frustrating.

But it was difficult because she was so sweet. Birmingham City was literally in the middle of nowhere in those days, before the area was built up – there were no shops – and every day she would bring me in pâté sandwiches. I absolutely hate pâté but I didn't have the heart not to eat them. And I kept her as long as I could, but in the end she had to go.

I decided to ask someone senior at the club to deal with it for me. 'It breaks my heart to have to get rid of her, and I know that if I try to do it I will end up keeping her. Would you do it for me?'

'No problem at all,' he said, and we agreed that once he had done it he would call me into his office so I could have a word with her. I could see them in the room opposite, talking, and after a while he waved me in. But as I sat down, he said, 'Karren has some bad news for you.' He hadn't done it. Instead, he had waited for me.

'Actually,' I said, 'I have something to tell you *both*.' My secretary was now not the only one in that room about to lose her job. And that taught me a lesson – when you need some dirty work done, do it yourself.

It was not pleasant, but I needed the right team in place. I could see so much potential in the club and David and I were brimming with ideas. We were doing something we loved, working on something that other people loved and that we could genuinely make better. At the time, the Premier League had only just been established, which was a fantastic opportunity.

Another change, which was perhaps more visible to the fans, was the kit. Birmingham City is known as the Blues, but the kit the team played in was green, orange and white. I couldn't see the logic. Within three days of taking over, I had changed the kit back to blue. The supporters were happy, which showed in the shop takings which, unsurprisingly, went up. When I took over we were selling fewer than 300 shirts a year; within a few years we were selling more than 30 thousand. Even armchair supporters were buying shirts as we promoted the club more and more.

A new start also meant that some ways of doing things came to an end, much to people's disappointment and annoyance. One incident that really took the biscuit was when I popped into the club's shop and spotted a stand-alone cash till. 'What's that doing there?' I enquired. It transpired that one of the players had his own shop area, where he sold his goods and kept the money. I couldn't believe it. He was selling all sorts of tat, mixed merchandise and items that he got free from club sponsors. Enterprising he might have been, but also way out of line. I simply pulled the plug of the till out of the wall, picked it up, walked out of the shop with it and threw it into the skip that was in the car park. And that put an end to that.

There were, of course, more fundamental problems to fix than could be sorted out with a change of kit and stopping a cheeky player's business on the side. Birmingham had lost its way and was attracting average gates – the number of people who come to a match – of just six thousand. The business model was fatally flawed. The club was associated with a hooligan element, which meant that the previous owners had set up a membership club. All well and good in theory, but in reality it meant that if you wanted to go and watch Birmingham play on a Saturday you had to have joined the membership scheme on the previous Thursday. It wiped out all the impulse match-goers and emphasised the negative aspect of the club's reputation, so people didn't want to bring their families through the gates.

And reputation in business is so important. Big brands and customers want to be associated with winners and companies that stand for something. This proved something of a conundrum for me back in 1993. Competition was fierce. Less than a mile away, Aston Villa was a fantastic club with great facilities doing well in the league. A few miles from them, Wolverhampton Wanderers was another well-run club with better facilities than ours. And, a few miles from them, West Bromwich Albion, again, at the time, was bigger and better. And there we were, with no identity and on the verge of relegation. Our grounds were run down, even falling down – some areas had actually been closed and condemned for safety reasons! – with very little seating, so the fans had to stand up.

What could we promote? We couldn't say we were the best-run club in the league because we were in administration. We couldn't say, 'Come to St Andrew's, our stadium and the facilities are good,' because they weren't. We couldn't even say, 'Come for the football,' because we were at the bottom of the table. And what to do about the competition all around us from bigger players? I knew, of course, that the value of the club was all about building a brand. Brands create value. But how do you get one with such a bad reputation?

First I worked out what we did have. We were an inner-city club. We had a large, young conurbation around us; we had a history of support. We also understood that young people and family entertainment represented the way forward. So I looked at what other leisure industries were doing, imagined what I'd want to do if I had a family and very little money, and looked across to the USA and other countries to see how they did things there. Basically, I thought about nothing else.

The next step was that we embarked on a series of promotions and advertising, something no one in football had ever done in that way before. We were putting adverts in newspapers, and adverts on local radio. We were the first club to use billboard advertising to promote the 'Kids A Quid' deal we had invented, where the under-16s could come to football for a pound. It was hugely popular. We got involved with Cadbury and Ribena so all the kids who arrived at the ground got free sweets and free drinks. And we worked with our partners to change the image of the club very visibly: for example, we persuaded the shirt sponsor we'd inherited, Triton Showers, to replace the toilets in the family area.

We also announced deals such as the lone-parent offer, where a single mother or father could come to football with two kids for a fiver. Then there was the school-dinners deal. We realised that the parents of kids who had free school dinners were on the poverty line and could never afford such luxuries as football tickets for their kids. So, we made sure that those kids who had free school dinners in and around Birmingham and wanted to come to football now could – for nothing. Suddenly gates started to creep up and the atmosphere in the ground changed, as the supporters discovered we were doing something for them and the community. We couldn't compete on facilities, but we could stand for something far more important: the heart and soul of Birmingham, bringing people together and, as a football club, being part of the community.

In business terms, that meant our database of supporters was increasingly the most valuable property the club had. I put in place a marketing department to make the best use of it and we came up with a series of imaginative letters to get people to renew their season ticket. I remember one showed a picture of people having blood transfusions with blue blood – the Blues, you see – pumping through their veins, while another had a picture of a bored-looking man in a busy shopping centre carrying bags for his wife, alongside a picture of a football crowd with the slogan 'Which crowd would you rather be in this Saturday?' It was all a way to get our supporters to become or stay part of the club and buy a season ticket. It worked. I had inherited a few thousand season-ticket holders and increased it to 23 thousand.

Overall, we built up a mailing list of nearly 100 thousand known supporters, combining current season-ticket holders, ex-season-ticket holders, match-day ticket buyers, people who had bought goods in our retail outlets – you name it. It was almost at the point that if you'd ever walked past the grounds you'd probably have had a letter dropping on your mat. Before we arrived, no supporters had ever been mailed. I'd make sure we mailed them four times a year and, more importantly, that every supporter got a Christmas card from the team. It meant we could promote special offers to our 100 thousand known supporters within just a few days. On my first Christmas at the club we launched Christmas and Grand National prize draws to our mailing list, making a profit of more than £60,000. I also re-launched the club's end-of-season dinner, which drew more than 1,500 people and sponsors to Birmingham's NEC venue, bringing in more than £100,000 profit in aid of our youth academy.

It was always about looking for a way to make things work better, seeing an opportunity and grasping it. That's why in the late 1990s we were one of the first clubs to embrace the Internet and use it as a vehicle to promote the club. I realised there was not much money to be made out of the Internet (other than the web shop), so I sold 10 years' revenue on our non-web-shop traffic for an upfront, non-refundable advance of more than £4 million. That was a vast amount of money to a Championship side. In the end, the company never brought in enough money to cover the advance, but it didn't really matter – we had been paid and could use the money to change and improve the club. That was my first multimillion-pound deal and it was the best in football, at the time, by a very long way.

That was later. But back at the start things began to change quickly. At that time the Anglo-Italian Cup drew an average gate for a game of about two thousand people. One great success was a game against Genoa when we managed a gate of 38 thousand because of our promotions: Kids A Quid, and a free pint of Carlsberg (courtesy of the commercial deal I had done with the brewery) for every adult who got there an hour before kick-off. The stadium was rammed. When I opened the paper the following day I saw the gates for the other games in that competition that evening. Some had had 1,200, others 700 – against our *38,000*. Even *Gazzetta dello Sport*, an Italian newspaper, bore the headline: '38,000 for the Anglo-Italian Cup'!

Having a bit of success with our strategy then brought its own new – welcome – challenges. I was keen to attract more families but, as we were getting big crowds, I had to limit the number of offers and free tickets. So I decided we should make the most of reserve games, switching them from the training ground to St Andrew's and calling them Family Fun Nights. We'd have face painting, a fire engine for the kids to sit in, a local fair putting on a few rides and a penalty shoot-out with the coaches in the car park. It took off. We regularly had 20 thousand attending, more than most clubs were getting for league games. The shop takings went up, the bar takings went up and – most importantly – our standing in the community and among our supporters went up. We were on our way. We had created something different, something new and exciting, and put the sparkle back into the club.

Before, there had been no understanding that the stadium was a commodity, that you mustn't ever miss an opportunity to sell. I would tell the sales staff: 'There are at least 23 events going on here this year, and they're called football matches, and our job is really simple. Our job is to sell out on every one. Because once the game has gone the opportunity to earn from that game has gone for ever.'

And we got things done. I have always believed that people should do the things that need to be done, when they need to be done, whether they like it or not, and that is about a can-do approach. David and I worked on ideas morning, noon and night. We thought of different ways to do things, creating excitement while all the time trying to build a brand.

There's something else that's unique to football that has to be addressed when you're running a business in that world: the huge discrepancy in earnings. You have to be able to motivate the 18-year-old who earns 15 grand a year in the ticket office as well as the 18-year-old who earns 15 grand a week playing football. The key is to bring those two people, whose wages will never meet, into one organisation, make them both feel part of a team, motivate them and help them respect each other's opinions.

The way to do that is through communication. You lead change through your staff's hearts and minds. The mind is all about information and clarity: you tell them what you want to achieve, how you're going to do it and exactly what their role is in the journey. The heart is about passion and enthusiasm. You can't teach it, you can only breed it through energy, ideas and sparkle. So at Birmingham I made sure that everyone knew what the club was doing, why it was doing it and why it was important. Then I kept repeating and updating that message. I made sure that the 18-year-old footballer understood that without someone selling the tickets he would be playing in an empty stadium, and that the 18-year-old in the ticket office understood that without the footballer there would be no tickets to sell. It was about creating an environment where everybody had a role. Those roles could be very different, the pay could be vastly different, but every role was respected and every role was important. We were a team.

In the same vein, I integrated the entire business so everyone knew what everyone else was doing. So, Hospitality had a spell working in Accounting, Accounting worked in Retail, Retail worked in Ticket Sales, and Ticket Sales worked with the groundsmen. Everyone knew about every area of the business – what was wrong with it, what needed doing, who was in which role. In that way we started to change the culture of the business, which is one of the hardest things to do. We started to instil that can-do approach.

Beyond that, the rules of building a successful football club are the same as for any other business. There are three pillars without which you cannot build a business: planning, process and structure – where are we going, how are we going to get there, and what structure will deliver it? A successful business is about understanding that, making sure that everybody else does and that they all feel the same way about the company.

There's a misconception you sometimes have to address, too. Even though you're working for someone else you still need an entrepreneurial spirit, make no mistake, to keep an eye out for profit. What are the costs? How do we make money? What are the angles? How do we drive more revenue? It's about understanding the common purpose of the organisation. It's about creating people with the same attitude, the same care for the business, as the person at the top. Because if you run the commercial area of a business, you'll only make a success of it if you treat it as if it were your own. You have to become the MD of that commercial 'business'. And you treat it as a business by treating every penny of the company's money as if it were yours. You have to ask yourself, 'Am I investing this money in my business or am I wasting it?'

When I joined West Ham United years later, I spoke to someone running the commercial department and asked how much we spent a year on match-day hostesses for the corporate-hospitality areas. And I knew when I asked the question – would have put my life, my house and everything I own on it – that the person wouldn't know the answer, couldn't even guess at it. That wasn't right. If it had been their own business they would have known the answer – they would have known how much money was spent and would have spent all day ringing around to find a cheaper deal, a better solution, an improvement to the service, to make a positive impact on the bottom line. They would have cared about such things. That is the difference between the mentality of a great business and one that is just OK. And I didn't want an OK business. I still don't.

So, there was a lot to achieve at Birmingham and I was doing the work of 10 people. Yet those first few years, although they were among the hardest of my career, were also among the most rewarding. As a result of that hard graft, in my first year the club made a trading profit for the first time in its modern history. That was a huge thing for me because, as a young woman who had gone into football and found herself in the spotlight, I wanted to show I had the backbone to deliver. It was a very rapid turnaround and that was solely down to relentless energy.

The Birmingham City I left 16 years later, in 2009, was like a machine: it was well maintained and well operated. Everyone from the person on reception to the financial director could tell you where we were going – our purpose – how we were getting there, what we were doing and what was important to us. We had a culture and we stuck to it. It was a winning formula that everyone who worked there understood.

That didn't mean it was my job at Birmingham – or later at West Ham – to motivate the footballers. That's down to the manager, and it isn't easy. Motivating someone who earns £75,000 a week is always going to be tricky! But I play a part in creating a wider professional environment so that the players feel they belong to something important; then they will want to behave correctly and dress smartly as appropriate representatives of their boss and the business. You should always talk positively about your business. Never run it down. It's your career, which is your livelihood. Managers create the discipline, but the club creates the framework.

So the manager deals day to day with the footballers, but sometimes I'm called in to deal with problems that the manager can't resolve, with a contract, perhaps, an agent or the tax authorities. I've sat in rehab with one player, a police station with another. If a player's father has forged his son's signature on documents, bought cars or properties, then taken the lot to Nigeria, leaving the player almost bankrupt, the manager won't be able to help him. In the same way, I can't help a player if he can't score from a corner. The players know that if they have a serious problem we will help, either by putting them in touch with the best lawyers or by offering them the advice they need, because that is our job.

And sometimes it is my job to discipline players. One or two have failed drugs tests, appeared in the newspapers in a bad light or been in the wrong place at the wrong time. I say to them, 'In your mind, fast-forward the movie you're in, called *Your Life*, and see yourself out of contract at the end of the year with such a bad reputation that no one wants to touch you. Your England career has just finished and you're looking at playing somewhere up north in the second division. Is that where you want this movie to end? Or are you going to say, "I'm a professional, I have a job to do, it won't last for ever, so I'm going to dedicate my time to doing it to the best of my ability"? If so, now is the time to stop what you're doing and think about where you want this movie to end.' It tends to work.

Some players make me laugh. They swagger in with their diamond earrings and call me 'Miss Brady'. I have little chairs on the other side of my desk so that when they sit down, they're like great big daddy-long-legs, all gangly arms and legs. And I say, 'What's the problem? Why have you come to see me?' We deal with it and off they go. I have a reputation for being tough, but I'm always fair, and when someone who works for me has a problem I'll fight alongside them and stand up for them. If I don't agree with them, I'll tell them why, and they'll know that my decision is final. But if I do agree I'll support them whole-heartedly until we come to a conclusion. After disciplinary action has been taken, they can ultimately appeal to me. I believe they accept that I will stick to the facts and the rules, that I will explain the situation, and that I won't go for the biggest penalty without reason.

I've got the routine down pat, by now. They'll come in and say, 'Miss Brady, I didn't know if I got a red card I'd be fined.'

'Well, is that your signature?' I ask.

'Yes,' they say.

'Well, your signature is on this document and it confirms you have read the rules about red cards and understand the consequences and fines.'

Then they'll say, 'I didn't know what I was signing as I didn't read it.'

To which I'll reply, 'Do you honestly expect me to believe that? Because that's actually a worse crime.'

'Is it?' they'll ask, getting a bit nervous.

'Are you telling me, a person of your age, that you'll sign anything someone puts in front of you without even thinking about it?'

Then the penny drops and they understand what being a professional footballer is all about. They never repeat the mistake.

I am certainly not as damning about footballers as Lord Sugar, who once said that most of them would be in prison if they hadn't become footballers. But then there is a big difference between me and Alan on this: he has fallen out of love with football, whereas I haven't. The game gave him a very hard time. Unjustifiably so. The Spurs supporters he was faced with as chairman didn't realise that they were chasing out of the club the very man who would save it. The very man who had the ideas, the energy and the business sense to sort it out, which he did. A man with a unique combination of business intelligence and passion for the club. Supporters just didn't see that. They misunderstood him and it ended badly. Some elements of the press picked on him too.

Funnily enough, it was because of this that we became friends. I felt he had been mistreated and said so in my *Sun* column at the time. He phoned and thanked me and we've been friends ever since. He's over the whole thing now, and I think he wishes he could do it all again with the benefit of hindsight. But people will never know the sacrifices he made for that club or the path he carved out for it that led to its success in 2011. I am convinced that everything it has going for it now leads back to Alan's time in charge.

Anyway, I don't think footballers are all bad. After all, I married one! Many of them just need very clear advice, very clear decisions and very clear direction. They are no more complicated than that. Some may let you down, and sometimes their actions seem unforgivable. But that's human nature.

Where Alan and I do agree 100 per cent is on football agents. Some are very good, but many are not. Often they provide no service to the player beyond getting them the move to a particular club, and most of the young players who come to us on very high wages need help and guidance. They need support so that others can't manipulate them, and they need help to prepare for retirement after their brief sporting careers. But, typically, an agent takes them up to Newcastle or wherever, says, 'Thank you very much,' pockets their fee, drops them off and leaves. Suddenly the player is in an unfamiliar place with nothing to do and no one to talk to. Is it any wonder that some go off the rails?

Of course, as well as the players and the agents, there's another set of people in the football world now. The game and the players have become increasingly glamorous during the years I've been involved, prompting the emergence of the WAGs – Wives And Girlfriends. Far be it from me to judge anybody – and, of course, some people would say that I'm a WAG myself, since I'm married to a footballer. I don't think there's any harm in loving your husband, looking good and dressing nicely, but going out with or marrying a footballer seems to be the limit of some women's ambition. It starts and stops there, which I think is very sad.

It concerns me that this is the dream for some young women, a life free of work and achievements but with all the trimmings. Wouldn't you get bored?! There's only so many times you can have your hair and nails done. I can't sit in a hairdresser's for longer than an hour, which is why I do it so rarely. I home-dyed my hair until I went grey at forty, as I couldn't be bothered with the fuss and preening. These women seem so vulnerable to me: they appear to have no independence and are reliant on a man saying, 'Here's some money. Go and buy a car.' Later, he may add, 'It'll be your car until I decide it's not.' That would be horrid. Plus, there's always a new model around the corner – and I'm not talking about cars!

Don't get me wrong, I'm not labelling women who marry footballers. I know Cheryl Cole – we appeared together on *Comic Relief Does The Apprentice* – and she is a truly lovely person. She's bright but not ruthless, and she's not fiercely ambitious. She knows she's got talent, but if she doesn't want to do something, no amount of 'This could lead to a huge sum of money' would ever persuade her to do it. When we were filming *The Apprentice* together she turned down the chance to be on *Britain's Got Talent*. Piers Morgan had put her forward but she decided it was not for her. I thought she'd be perfect but she wasn't sure and no amount of talking would persuade her. She's a woman with brains and beauty, and added to that is an inner strength that sets her apart.

I feel the same about Victoria Beckham, a successful businesswoman who has built a global brand with dogged determination. She makes time to run a business and bring up a family, a well-balanced one, and not many people in Hollywood can say that! And she does it with sophistication and elegance. You'll never see her falling out of a nightclub. I can't understand why she gets a hard time from the press. She's a role model. She looks good, dresses with style and has a lovely family. It's these things that people want to take from her, but she has held it all together, come what may. I take my hat off to her.

Sometimes it's odd to think that I'm seen as a role model too, the First Lady of Football, and all that. I can definitely pinpoint the time in my life when my public profile took off, other than the hoo-hah when I arrived at Birmingham. It was in 1997 when we floated Birmingham City on the stock market, which made me the youngest managing director of a public limited company (PLC) in the UK and boosted my profile as a businessperson.

I did the flotation in three months, largely on my own because we wanted to do it as cheaply as possible, so I learned a lot. I had a lawyer and a stockbroker to help and advise on fixed-price deals but I did all the documentation and prepared all the due diligence, which meant collecting all the information about the club, for the lawyer to check. I looked after every little detail myself. So I would put something in the documents, like 'Birmingham City Football Club is based less than a mile away from the city centre,' and the lawyer would say, 'How do you know it's less than a mile from the city centre?' This was pre-Internet so I would have to get into my car, find the point that the map said was the city centre and drive there to measure it. Lo and behold, it was 0.82 miles. The process was literally that laborious.

Then I had to go out selling the shares across the City, which was something completely new to me. I did it as a one-woman band and had to pull out all my energy, passion and enthusiasm for the business. When you're trying to sell your dream to someone else, to ask them to invest in it, it really focuses the mind: you have to work out how to deal with the criticism. To deal properly with all the questions you have to be thoroughly prepared and understand all aspects of what you're doing. You also have to accept that not everybody is going to believe in the same things that you do.

We were a small business, raising a very small amount of money, and we thought people would say, 'Sorry, can't be bothered,' but actually they were intrigued by us. They liked the story of the club, and they were interested in me too. I don't think the City had met anyone quite like me before. Perhaps they thought, Oh, for a million quid might as well have a bit of fun, but they believed I would do what I said I would.

And I did. I'm proud to say that the people who backed our vision, the people who bought shares when we floated on the stock market, doubled their money when we sold out. And the people who supported a rights issue – when we issued additional shares – *quadrupled* their money. But the really lucky investors were those who were there when we arrived. David Sullivan and his business partner, David Gold, had only bought 80 per cent of the club, and back then the shares were valued at under 1p each. When I sold the club in 2009 the shares went for £1 each, so some people got 100 times their money. How many investments can boast that, let alone any investment in football?

So, the spotlight was shining more and more on me and I suppose that gave me a sense of how high profile I was becoming, but for me it was still all about the business. I still had a board to serve and I knew I was doing it for them. And I now had a responsibility to the shareholders: I had to ensure that the business was well run, go to the City every year and announce our results, hold AGMs and present the company accounts. Although he was my chairman, David Sullivan allowed me to chair the meetings, yet again putting great trust in me, but I was the one who could answer all the questions raised. I thrived on the detail: I had to know everything, from a query about a nail found under a seat right through to complex financial matters.

And I think that, if you look at most good companies, you find that the person at the top knows every little thing about that business.

Considering how brand-aware I am, and how much I enjoy developing brands, it is odd that I didn't realise then that I was becoming a brand myself. But I think, like most women, I served the company before I served myself. I just didn't think about myself like that. The flotation was a huge turning point for me, but I didn't know it at the time. In fact, it was another ten years before I started thinking about Karren Brady, rather than Karren Brady, Birmingham City Football Club. The flotation started that process, but didn't finish it.

What followed were achievements like winning Business-woman of the Year, being invited to lunch by the Queen, receiving my honorary doctorate from Birmingham University – I am Dr Karren Brady! All of it added up to recognition of my hard work and was hugely rewarding. And then there was the sale of Birmingham City for £82 million in November 2009.

That sale might well have been the end of the story for me and football. After all, I had devoted over 16 years to the business, and I had lots of other professional interests, in retail, the media, *The Apprentice*, public speaking, and so on. But within three months, David Sullivan and David Gold had bought West Ham, and there I was, on my way to sort out another football club.

The journey had started again.

CH.5
MY LIFESTYLE
MONEY, FAME ... HARD WORK

You might wonder how, with this sort of workload, I've spent my free time. After all, it can't all be work and no play, as they say. And success has brought me some wonderful things. A lovely home for my family, enough money for the things I want to buy, a degree of choice over what I say yes to, and the chance to do interesting work and meet fascinating people.

But when I read articles about the lives of successful women, which make them seem like one long shopping trip down Bond Street, followed by lunch with famous friends at a chichi restaurant and then back with the chauffeur to the office where a personal masseur awaits, I just laugh. My life is nothing like that – and neither would I want it to be.

The truth is that the more successful you become, the harder you work, because the more successful you become, the more work you're offered. It is a self-perpetuating cycle.

Nowadays I have many jobs. As well as my 'day job', managing West Ham United Football Club, I am a non-executive director of Arcadia, which owns Top Shop, and a consultant for Simon Cowell's company Syco. I have my personal businesses, including writing newspaper columns and public speaking; I represent various charities and other organisations; and, of course, there is *The Apprentice*, which we film for several weeks a year. To fit all of this in, I work pretty much constantly.

No two days are the same but, at the moment, since much of my work is in London and my home is in Birmingham, my week is divided into two. Most Mondays start with me catching a train south. Then I try to spend four days working very hard in London and three nights, including the weekends, with my family in Birmingham. I usually go home on Thursday night, but that isn't the end of my working week. In theory, weekends are for the family, but in reality it is never as clear-cut as that. If West Ham are playing on a Saturday or Sunday, I travel to most of those matches, and I am always at the end of my BlackBerry.

When I'm in London I work constantly, every minute of the day. I don't stop for lunch, I don't go to the gym. I work from the moment I wake up until the moment I go to sleep. I'm not exaggerating. The first thing I do when I open my eyes is check my emails. I work on the way to and from the office, and in the evenings I set up dinners, which are really meetings, with people I need to see, or attend business functions. I once worked out that if I drank less water I could use the toilet less, which meant

I could fit more into my day, as it was a long walk to the ladies from my office. How sad is that!

So the idea that I have little moments of indulgence, that I have a private yoga instructor coming in or someone to do my nails, is just fantasy. That is why it's so important to like what you do – otherwise you'd be in a permanently bad mood!

In a way, the intensity of how I work now is like going back 20 years. When I first went to Birmingham City I worked every minute of the day and late into the night: when you're on the way to where you want to be, it's a test of your endurance. How much can you take on and get through? Nobody got successful leaving work at five o'clock – unless you own oil wells or inherited your money.

I've passed the endurance test now, and one benefit is that I feel more able to say no. You have to ration your time. When I was younger and forging ahead in my career, if someone asked me to go to a dinner or a function, I would feel I had to say yes, that it must be important, and then I'd spend a week trying to think of ways to get out of it because, actually, I didn't want to go. And then if I did go and didn't get what I thought I would in return, I came away feeling resentful.

Over the years I've learnt that you've got to say yes when you mean yes, and no when you mean no. If you say yes for good reasons – because you want to go to or do whatever it is and expect nothing in return – then you limit your expectations: you enjoy the event or task more, and you get more benefit from it. Now I say yes only to things I want to do, or things I know are vital. I think being able to choose what you say yes or no to is one of the great rewards of success.

Still, I'm not quite there yet. Although I have passed the endurance test and can now say no to a lot of things, my time is not my own. And it's not just because there are a lot of things I want to say yes to. I read something once about the founders of Google, who said that one of the toughest things about running a business is that you don't run your own diary. That is so true.

Every night my PA tells me where I'm going the next day, who I'm seeing, what I'm doing, and that's my life. I can't say, 'Well, actually, you know what? I'm not going to go and see the Government to talk about the Olympic Stadium, I'm going to do something else.' You're constantly on an agenda and it's not always your own.

The founders of Google decided that the only way to resolve this was to sack their PAs so that nothing could be put in their diaries. I'm not going to sack my PA, but I thought it was an interesting concept. A point comes when you're really successful and you finally do what you want to do, rather than doing what needs to be done, and that idea is very attractive. But I'm not quite there yet.

One of the other great benefits of professional success is, of course, money. I have reached the point where I don't have to look at the price of anything, within reason. I have a lovely home in the West Midlands, a Bentley, a flat in Knightsbridge and I fly first class. If I want something, I no longer have to go without something else. I don't have to worry about how I'm going to pay my children's school fees. If I want to go on holiday I ring my PA and say I want to go to the Maldives in two weeks' time – please find me the best hotel. Obviously, she'd look for the best deal because I don't like wasting money, but she doesn't need to.

Yet money has never been my driving force. I have never lain awake at night thinking, I need money. Independence has always been a much more important motivator. After all, I definitely would have done things differently if money had been my number-one priority. On two occasions I have been offered massive jobs that would have paid me far more than I was earning at the time, but that wasn't enough to sway me. Both were based in Los Angeles, but my kids are at school and their life is here in the UK. That was more important than either of those jobs.

I think my attitude towards money comes from having had a good upbringing in a safe environment. When I was a young child, before my dad became successful, we were a long way from being rich, but I never remember going without anything. There was always enough.

When I read David Gold's book, or Alan Sugar's, I realise that, for some people, the motivation must be very different. Those men grew up with very little and they want to be sure they will never be in that position again. My kids would have no idea if we were struggling or seriously wealthy, and I think that's important. I want them to feel entirely safe, even as I also believe in encouraging them to work. My daughter gets £40 a month pocket money and somehow she manages to get all the things she wants out of me without spending any of it! My son, on the other hand, is one of those people who spends every penny as soon as he gets it. But he spends to accumulate. He has a doughnut business: he buys them in bulk from the supermarket and sells them individually at school to pupils and teachers. He's always got a scheme on the go!

I don't want to give the impression I haven't enjoyed my money. When I was younger I made a promise to myself that, until I was 25, I would spend every penny I earned, and I did. I enjoyed luxury holidays, I drove a Porsche, and all my clothes were from Chanel and Valentino. But I told myself that, once I was 25, I would save more than I spent, and that's how I live now. It's important when you're young to enjoy your money, because once you start a family your responsibilities and commitments take over. That's why I'm so cautious with my savings and am really against get-rich-quick schemes. I work too hard for my money to gamble it on anything I don't believe in.

In the same way, when I buy something, I'm aware of how much work I had to do to earn it. And if I see people with lovely things I feel really pleased for them – I don't think, God, I've got to go out and get one of those. I'm just not a jealous person – I never have been. At boarding school, everyone used to borrow my things and I didn't care. I could be generous because none of those things labelled or defined me.

Of course I never feel deprived. If I wanted to go into Chanel and buy two coats, three handbags, four suits and spend 25 grand, I could, but I wouldn't. Often the celebrities you see who are flash with their money are people who have grown up with very little. They need the trappings to say to the world, 'I've got money, don't you know?' They want to treat themselves. But that's not me.

I do have my indulgences. I still really like Chanel. I don't buy the clothes often because in the main, they don't suit me, but I like the accessories – a laptop case, a handbag, the jewellery. When I've done a really big deal, I'll go there and buy something. Every time I use it, it reminds me of the fun of the deal, the plans I pulled off.

Lots of other luxuries, I'm not bothered about. I don't mind a massage, but I'm usually too busy to enjoy it. If I go to the hairdresser, I often walk out with my hair wet because I can't stand how long it takes. If I'm in a lovely restaurant, I want to eat and go; I don't get dressed up and I don't want to be there for two hours. As I've acquired money and experience, I find that, when I go out to eat, it's because I'm hungry. I might choose a café or a five-star restaurant – but what I want is to be fed.

And there's nothing I hanker for. One of the important lessons I've learnt in life is that the things you think will solve your problems often become your problems. People dream about owning a house in France so that they can go there any time to relax. Well, nice idea, but you'll probably be too busy to go there. Or, when you arrive, the pool's broken down, or the air-conditioning won't work, so your lovely home in France becomes just another problem. Often with such trappings, the best day is the day you buy them, and the next-best day is the day you sell them.

Something I do consider worth spending money on is luxury holidays. And that is because, more than anything else, those are the times when I can relax. For 13 years I didn't have a holiday and barely took a day off. I just worked solidly. If you want to be successful, that is what you have to do. A career is built on sheer hard work – endurance and tolerance, relentless energy, the constant battle between kids and work. You can't just stop when you're tired, you have to push on.

When I was young I had relentless energy going spare but, as you get older, your batteries go flat a lot more quickly, and you need to be able to recharge them. I never have a lie-in, a late breakfast or even a day with no agenda, but occasionally I think that would be nice, and occasionally I think I need that. The answer for me is holidays.

Because I do burn out. The importance of my health and wellbeing really hit home after I had to have brain surgery, in February 2006. Not often, but occasionally, I reach the point where I just have to stop, and it happens more often as I get older. The problem is that often I can't stop, not even for a day, and if I'm not careful I end up in a vicious circle: there are things I have to do when I would like to be doing something else because I'm exhausted, but I've got to keep going and become yet more tired and hungry for a break. That's when life starts to get less satisfying.

For me, that's why holidays are so important. Now I take holidays regularly and I really look forward to them. The pause in routine is so precious – there's no diary, so I don't have to be here or go there. It's a complete break. I have one main holiday a year, and perhaps a couple of others, although never for more than a week and I always have my BlackBerry with me. I'm shocked that some people can be out of reach in the evenings, or at weekends, or on holiday. I am always contactable. I try to keep family time clear but it isn't realistic to have no contact at all with work, and my children understand – they're well trained! And they can see the benefits of my hard work.

It's not ego; I do need to be reachable because something really important might be happening. Very often it's the little things that can change the course of the business. And I believe that if there's a crisis I need to be involved because the essence of that business is in my DNA. Everybody operates as I want them to operate and therefore, if they need me, I've got to be available for them. That isn't a chore: I would be furious if I wasn't kept informed.

Having said that, I may tweak the arrangement when I'm on holiday. When David Sullivan is on holiday, he does his emails in the morning and again at five o'clock, keeping the afternoon clear. Maybe that's a better idea than being constantly on call.

Now and again something comes up that someone else could deal with and just notify me but, because I'm available, I find myself sorting it out. Before I know it, an hour and a half's gone by.

People might expect me to be all go-go-go on holiday, up at the crack of dawn to scale the Pyramids or canoe down the Amazon, given the pace of my working life. They couldn't be more wrong. A great holiday to me is about luxury, about being somewhere hot and with great service. It's about being with my family, which is more important than ever as the children get older and I am away more.

I'm always exhausted when I get there and I want to be indulged. I'm not a backpacker and I don't want to see if I can walk up a mountain. I'm not a great sightseer. For me the greatest luxury is to have no need to be anywhere. I don't even want to dress for dinner. I just want to hang loose.

I'm the same back home, really. I was asked in an interview recently, 'Where is the most romantic place you have ever had a meal?' I said, 'In my living room, because I don't get to be there very often.' I'm not attracted to the celebrity lifestyle, seeing and being seen at designer restaurants. I'm a business-woman and a mother in my forties: my favourite way to relax is to go to bed early and watch a film. Driving around in limos, falling out of nightclubs, that's not me. Never has been.

Because of *The Apprentice*, I get invited to TV awards ceremonies and other events, but I go to hardly any of them. The idea of sitting next to someone from *EastEnders* is not my cup of tea. I'm not a party animal and never was – those all-night outings when I was 14 were more about doing what I wanted, having a few adventures and proving my independence. And even when I'm invited to an event that appeals to me – when maybe I do feel like getting dressed up – I usually can't go! I've got a job, I've got two children, and these things take up all of my time.

I've even turned down the Oscars because it would have meant four days away from my business and my kids, and I just can't do that. Not that it was a great sacrifice to miss it, but I would have been interested to try it once. A woman once said that life is divided into work, children and social life, and you only have time for two of the three. I agree. So, I go to the events my children will enjoy. We all went to a couple of the *Harry Potter* premieres, for example, and that was great. We went to see Justin Bieber too, which might not have been my first choice – spending an evening with 15 thousand screaming teenage girls – but when you're a parent, everything is about what your kids want to do. One of my best nights out recently was the *Twilight: Breaking Dawn* premiere with my daughter Sophia, who looked so beautiful. In fact, she's started modelling and acting now – God help me!

The sort of events I do enjoy for myself and say yes to include anything political. If I had a choice between accompanying Brad Pitt or David Cameron, I'd choose David Cameron every time. I really enjoy giving a talk at Downing Street, and have done so several times.

Politicians are usually much nicer than people think. I thought Gordon Brown was a man of integrity – thoroughly honest – and his wife, Sarah, is a lovely person, all about family and loyalty, a woman of intelligence and personality. I like David Cameron also and think he's got a certain style. He's tried to find a balance between his background and that of the general public and to merge those two things, an interesting approach. In the future, I would like to help the Government in some way. I'm a Tory and believe that success in running the country is based on the same tenets as running a business: process, planning and strategy. In fact, I think I would be good in politics and one day may well take up the mantle. It has always been an ambition of mine.

That said, I admire people right across the political spectrum. David Blunkett was another politician who stood out for me. Politics is a difficult game, because we ask our politicians to be open and honest and, when they are, the press slaughter them for their opinions. So all we get are these non-conversations, because they're just playing it safe all the time. But David Blunkett is one of those old-style leaders who says what he thinks and, as a plain speaker myself, I like that. Alex Salmond is the same. We had a great lunch once and he has my admiration. As do Andrew Mitchell, David Lammy, Lyn Brown and Boris Johnson. All of these people have one thing in common: they would make a decision that would benefit the country, however unpopular, over the considerations of PR and making sure they got the next election's vote. That to me is the true mark of a real politician.

The Queen has invited me for lunch twice, and that was truly special. When you're introduced to her, they announce what you do, and in my case it was this and that and this and that, and the Queen said, 'Oh, my goodness, I don't know how you do it.' I said, 'Well, ma'am, I guess it's a bit like you – when you're a working mother, you've got to get on with it,' and we had a bit of a laugh. At one lunch I sat next to J. K. Rowling, another woman I admire very much. She is an author but also a fantastic businesswoman, a mother and a builder of world-class brands. Beautiful, too, and extremely elegant and understated.

We found ourselves sitting next to a businesswoman who was vulgar and obnoxious, rude to anyone and everyone in sight. Meanwhile J.K. and I sat there quietly: just two self-made ladies, running our businesses, running our families, not caring if anyone knew who we were – simply pleased to be there. Thrilled, in fact. She is definitely someone I would like to be friends with. I also made another friend that day in Kelly Hoppen, the interior designer, again a self-made lady I wanted to know.

However, generally, my husband Paul and I don't do glamorous things. At weekends we make dinner, sit around, watch the kids play sport, maybe have dinner with friends – my social life is pretty low-key. Most of my friends are friends that I've grown up with or who live nearby. I've known my best friend for 15 years, and our children are at school together. My oldest friend is someone I went to school with.

I do have a couple of high-profile friends. I've known Piers Morgan for years, since the days before he was a TV personality, and I really like him. He's funny and quite cheeky, and a very loyal friend. He and I were out together, watching Arsenal versus Birmingham, the day that, as editor of the *Mirror*, he published the photographs of British soldiers abusing an Iraqi that turned out to be fake. I felt so sorry for him that he had been duped by the pictures, which ultimately cost him his job. All he wanted to do was to be a newspaper editor. It was his whole life, and to have one career like that in a lifetime is a truly amazing accomplishment. But to go on and get an even bigger career, in Hollywood of all things, is an astonishing achievement. He's an undeniably good writer as well.

But I don't have lots of celebrity friends, and that's because I'm not a celebrity. I don't go on TV because I want to be famous, I'm a businessperson who goes on TV to talk about business or be part of a business show, as is the case with *The Apprentice*. I get requests all the time from different programmes – *Strictly Come Dancing*, *Celebrity Family Fortunes*, ice-skating and jungles. I even got asked to do *Ready Steady Cook* – bloody cheek. Do I look like the sort of person who would do

Ready Steady Cook? But I say no to everything, daytime TV or not. I have no ambitions at all to be on TV as a goal in itself.

I have tried that and just thought, No. Several years ago I did *Loose Women*, the panel show. I guess I thought it would be interesting, but it wasn't. I remember interviewing an actor I'd never heard of from *Holby City*, a programme I'd never watched, and just thinking, Why am I doing this? I'm asking you questions, but I don't care what the answers are. I'm not cut out for this. I left the following day.

I have noticed it is often the people who say, 'I'd never do TV, I'm a serious businessperson,' who then make an appearance as an expert and get a taste for it. You suddenly see them doing all sorts of shows that have nothing to do with business.

That's not me. I love *The Apprentice*, I admire and respect Alan Sugar, but I think it would be awful if you were on a show you didn't like or that didn't reflect who you are. *Strictly Come Dancing* would be that for me, waltzing around the floor in a sparkly frock with a pasted-on grin. I don't pretend to be one person and act another. What you see on *The Apprentice* is me, not me pretending to be somebody else. In doing it I'm still true to my essence, which is business. So if a small television station in Scotland asked me to go and present the morning programme, I'd laugh, but I know some people who would say, 'Yes, yes, yes.' If TV is your career I suppose you have to take every opportunity, but my career is business.

Besides, seeing yourself on TV is awful! To get to 42 and see your face on a 50-inch high-definition TV screen is a shocking moment. It's a bit like when you hear your voice on your own answer machine – you think, I don't sound like that, do I? Some people love watching themselves, but I certainly don't.

And my children hate the fame side of things. In London we're pretty anonymous, but if we go out shopping in Birmingham, people will come up and say, 'It's Karren Brady!' I've mastered the ability not to acknowledge my own name, because often people won't be sure if it's me or not so they'll just shout, 'Karren!' If I don't look up, they think, Oh, it can't have been her.

It intrigues me how far people will go to be famous – businesspeople posing in their underwear, that sort of thing. I really don't understand why anyone would be motivated by fame. In an ideal world I would have my media career but not be famous, but you can't have one without the other.

At heart, I'm a private person. I do like being part of something that's successful, and I want to be involved in shows where I can demonstrate my expertise, but then people feel they have the right to start commenting on me in a very personal way, which I hate.

It can be very sexist. Newspapers routinely ridicule women like Fern Britton, Nigella Lawson or me on the basis of our appearance – hasn't she put on weight? You can just picture the man making that decision, smoking his fags, 20 stone, on the picture desk. They make such a big deal about people who have lost weight, and anyone who's normal they just ridicule.

If someone doesn't like what I've said on *The Apprentice*, they'll write on a message board, 'Karren Brady, that fat cow'. They would never say that about Nick Hewer, my male counterpart on the show. They'd never say, 'Nick's put on weight,' or 'Nick's got eye bags,' or 'Nick's had Botox.' (By the way, and just for the record, Nick hasn't got eye bags and nor has he had Botox, and neither have I. After brain surgery the thought of injecting poison near my brain scares the hell out of me.)

There's this idea that if you're a woman and you put yourself out there, you've got to take on the chin whatever anyone wants to throw at you. But why? I'm a high-profile business-woman, not a celebrity. I don't pretend to be a model. I'll never bring out a fitness DVD, I can promise you that. I'm not publishing the Karren Brady diet. No one can say I'm being hypocritical. I run my business and I run it very well.

As for my weight, I've always been relaxed about it. I don't diet, I eat what I want – within reason – and don't worry about it. But it's different when you're in the public eye – and TV makes you look bigger than you are. There are times when I think, Oh, God, I look awful.

But I am not going to starve myself because other people on TV are thinner than me. Including Alan Sugar, who's shrinking! He sent me an email once saying he had done a 100-mile bike ride and I wrote back, 'For God's sake, eat something – I'm standing next to you on screen looking larger and larger.'

You just have to take the view that too much emphasis is placed on women's appearance. I make the most of myself, but I look how I look. I know I could lose weight if I wanted to – anyone can – but it's a case of, actually, how much energy can you put into that along with everything else? So I tell myself, You're fine, but if you got five pounds heavier it would be too much. And, as I've got older, I've learnt how to dress around it.

Scrutiny of your appearance tends to come hand in hand with another form of attention: the paps. I don't generally have problems with the paparazzi but I did get papped once, when I was on the beach in Mauritius, in a private area with my son. It could have been worse – I could have been in swimwear – but it was a horrible picture. The headline went along the lines of '£82 million in the bank and she can't afford sun cream,' as I had a sunglasses shape on my face. You try running around on your own playing football, swimming, canoeing, feeding the turtles, kayaking, then starting the whole thing again with a 12-year-old son and tell me you've got time to remember to sun-cream yourself after you've done him!

There is certainly a side to the media that's all about ridicule, which is unpleasant and embarrassing however thick-skinned you are – and I am thick-skinned. You get to a certain age when, if you're going to appear in the paper – especially on a beach – you want to have some control over how you look.

But the hardest thing is not what they say about you, or the pictures they use, but what they say or get wrong about other people who may be close to you. Even trivial-seeming details can have the potential to hurt. In one piece they said that my dad was in his seventies, when he's in his sixties. In another, they said my mother worked at Tesco. Both my parents were upset, which gave me more grief than anything that's written about me.

It can be unpleasant for the children, too. We were all coming back on the train from a West Ham match recently, and people were saying, 'Slag,' at me, and all sorts of horrible things. Of course, the children were shocked – they'd never heard anything like that before. You have to say to them, 'Look, there is the good and the bad and sometimes you have to deal with the bad, and this is part of it.' I have learnt to accept it because that's all I can do.

Of course, there are ways in which fame is great. It's great when you want to get into a booked-out restaurant or your children want to go to the *Harry Potter* film set and meet the actors. I'll fully admit that I'm like anybody else – I like it when I like it, and I don't like it when I don't like it. I don't like it when I'm in Sainsbury's, and people come up to me to say, 'Oh, by the way, West Ham are shit.' Who would?

That's the problem with fame – you can't have the great stuff without the bad stuff. Once you're out there, you're really out there. There's no putting the genie back in the bottle.

CH.6
MY HOME LIFE
HAVING IT ALL?

By now, it must be pretty evident that when I'm not working my life is all about my family. Yet I really never thought I would get married. I always wanted to have children, certainly, but the plan when I was younger was to do it on my own, not with a partner.

I just didn't want a man telling me what to do, didn't think I could share my life with anyone, and wasn't really interested in what anyone would be able to offer. Looking back, I sound like Howard Hughes! As usual, I didn't want anyone having any control over me, interfering with my way of doing things or my decisions. But that was because I'd never been in love and never met anyone I wanted to share my life with.

To my surprise, that changed when I moved to Birmingham at 23. I was ready to work, not to find a boyfriend. I knew no one in the city, never having set foot there until we arrived to take over the football club. More than that, turning Birmingham City around was a huge undertaking that involved working every hour of the day. At night I would be stranded in a hotel in the middle of nowhere, rather than clubbing and pubbing, like many other women in their early twenties. So, I certainly wasn't looking to fall in love – but even if I had been, the odds of it happening under those circumstances would not have seemed high.

As for a falling in love with a footballer, I would have laughed in your face if you'd suggested such a thing to me. I'd once said that footballers are only interested in drink, clothes and the size of their willies. But one of the first players I met at Birmingham was Paul Peschisolido, and I found myself eating my words.

From the start, I thought Paul was good-looking and obviously a really nice guy – not a Jack the lad or flash at all. He kept himself to himself. Paul is from Canada, so he was on his own in Birmingham, and all my friends were in London, which might as well have been Canada for all the time I got to spend with them. So we were in the same boat.

Now, during that time, I had to go to some event every night – children's certificates to hand out, charity dos, fêtes. It was part of my job, and soon Paul was volunteering to come with me. We ended up spending a lot of time together and I really liked him. We just clicked. On one occasion, I remember, he was injured after a game, and on my way home I popped into the hospital to see him. I got there at about eight and I was there until two in the morning, just talking. We weren't together, not a couple, but it was clear we got on well and I was in that stage of trying to work out if he liked me back.

Then one day I was sitting at my desk with a bad headache, probably from working all those 16-hour days, and a friend phoned. 'You like that Paul Peschisolido, don't you?' she said.

'Yes,' I said, wondering where this was going.

'Have you seen the paper?' Sure enough, there was this big article about Paul and how he was making a name for himself. All great for him and the club – except there was all this stuff about a girlfriend back in Canada, and how he was missing her. Not so great for me. There was even a picture of the woman, and I just thought, Shit.

I grabbed my keys and told my secretary I was going back to the hotel where I lived, that I felt ill and needed to go to bed. That article had been the last straw on top of my splitting head. Just as I was pulling into the car park, my phone rang. I checked who was calling: Paul. 'Hi,' he said.

'Yeah?' Not too friendly, I was tired and pissed off.

'I just wanted to let you know that the reporter got completely the wrong end of the stick. The relationship with that woman's over.'

A straight talker, like me. Paul hadn't needed to call. Nothing had happened between us; we were still just friends – I was still in that 'Does he like me?' stage. But he did call, and that made me think, Maybe he does like me. Suddenly I felt a lot better. And after he'd given me that signal, if you like, we quickly went from being friends to being a couple. So perhaps that's the one occasion I can thank a journalist for getting things wrong!

Things moved fast and within eighteen months of meeting we were married. We had a baby eleven months after that, and we're still together over sixteen years later. I've never looked back. I can absolutely put my hand on my heart and say the day I die I'll still be married to Paul, unless he dies before me. I'm not particularly religious, but I believe in my marriage: I would never divorce, and if Paul died, I would never remarry. I could never do it again. Nonetheless, a few months ago, the *Daily Express* was adamant we had separated and were heading for a divorce and phoned him to ask if I had left him. 'Well,' he said, 'She was all right this morning at breakfast, but with Karren you never know!' Laughter is the key.

Why has it worked? The most fundamental thing about Paul is that he is a good person. He's committed and honest, not devious or ruthless. He's very calm too, which is good for me, because I'm so full on. And he has, at his core, rock-solid beliefs in family values, honesty and decency, all of which are important to me. As a Catholic – as am I – he has strong religious values, which I think is quite wholesome in a man. And, most importantly, I like him, and I don't want to share him with anyone else.

I've noticed over the years that we're well suited in other ways, too. Working in football – although it's not confined to football – I know a lot of men who are very needy, who want to be told, 'You're the best, you're wonderful, and you're marvellous.' Paul isn't like that. I would hate to be with a sensitive soul: I just haven't got time. Likewise, I don't need anyone to say to me, 'You're marvellous, you're wonderful, you're fantastic, what would we do without you?' I'm low-maintenance – I know I'm doing a good job under very difficult circumstances and that's enough. Paul understands that and he supports me by just letting me get on with it.

So Paul is not romantic – he doesn't even know florists have been invented – but he'll often go and fill my car with petrol early on a Monday morning when I'm in the shower, before he goes to work, as he knows I have to drive to London. And we don't need grand gestures to know that we're each other's backbone. We have very different personalities, but we complement each other perfectly, as well as understanding the things we can't change, like our shared stubborn streak. By now, I've given up telling Paul how he should do something, and he has given up telling me why I should do something!

I trust him with my life – and that trust extends into every area of our life together. He will never say, 'Where are you going tonight? What time will you be home?' and I never question him like that either. I know that whatever he's doing he's got to do, and I know he's not doing anything that he would be ashamed of me knowing about. Which is something to appreciate, I know. I've got friends who tell me their husbands won't let them see their mobile phones and I just think. If there's something on your mobile phone that you wouldn't be happy for your husband or wife to see, there's something happening that shouldn't be happening. And that's not right.

Paul just isn't like that. I knew from the start that he was family-oriented, and he's a really fantastic father. That's not a surprise to me, as he comes from a lovely, warm family. They spend every holiday with us, have spent their lives helping us and have been a constant support throughout my time with Paul. I would not part with them for a king's ransom. They are wonderful people and, frankly, my life would not be the same without them. I adore his mother, Julie, who's the most fantastic person and has been an amazing help to me with my children and my career. She truly is a second mother to me.

Fortunately for me, she raised Paul to respect women. When we were first together, we were going out on Valentine's Day, and Paul was talking to Julie on the speakerphone in his car, although she didn't know I could hear. He told her something I'd done, and she said, 'I think you might be out of your depth there. She sounds like Superwoman.' It was very funny – but he has never been fazed by me or my career.

The respect goes two ways, of course. I remember the first time we went to Canada to meet his family, in the summer of

1994. We were living together by then, with him the star of the team and me the managing director of Birmingham City, but still we weren't allowed to sleep in the same bedroom. And, in a funny way, I liked that. We got engaged that weekend, so it certainly didn't throw a spanner in the works. He proposed to me in front of his family – not on one knee – and then we went for dinner. The two of us didn't earn a lot of money back then, so his parents sent us away for a weekend to Niagara Falls, which was lovely.

Of course, our jobs meant that it wasn't just family who had – in their case, fair enough – opinions on how we should conduct our relationship. One morning, soon after we'd got together, the postman knocked on my door and said, 'There's a photographer hiding in the bush.'

I was just amazed – bear in mind, this was 1994, before the paparazzi showed much interest in me. 'Are you sure?' I said.

'Yes.' He nodded. 'There's definitely a photographer hiding in the bush.'

Funny things happen when you get a public profile. I was so new to being in the papers that it hadn't occurred to me that strangers would be remotely interested in my relationship. After all, it wasn't as if we were having some illicit affair – Paul wasn't married; I wasn't married. We weren't even hiding it: our close friends knew we were together, including a few people at work. But that lurking photographer marked the start of it being all over the papers.

I didn't like the way they painted it at all. I think the media made a mistake about our relationship, thinking that I was just sleeping with one of the players – which I was, of course – but failing to understand that we were more serious than that. The way we dealt with it was to come out, effectively. We didn't issue a press release – 'Paul and Karren are together'; I can't imagine anything worse – but we did tell everyone. And the photographers could sneak around trying to take grainy photos of us and portray it as some dirty affair, but we were in love.

We were married in June 1995. We had our first child, Sophia, in 1996, and our son, Paolo, two years later. So there – it was serious.

But for a while we were a story. Paul and I have never discussed the impact that had on him in the dressing room, but I don't think they gave him too hard a time. He was very popular. But I'll never know and it's a long time ago now.

As for me – well, I was the boss, so it didn't really affect me. I do remember Jack Wiseman, who was the vice-chairman of Birmingham at the time and a real traditionalist, talking to me about it. Jack was a really nice guy, and a big name in football, but I think he fundamentally believed that there was no place in football for women – before he met me anyway. When I first took over at Birmingham, he told David Sullivan, 'We don't have women in the boardroom,' and David said, 'Well, I'll leave you to tell Karren, if you're brave enough!'

When the story broke about me and Paul, Jack came into my office, sat down and said, 'I want to have a serious word with you.'

'Yes? What's the problem?'

'I understand you're having an affair with a footballer,' he said.

'What's it got to do with you?'

'Well,' he said, 'you have to be careful. You're in a privileged position. Who are you having an affair with?'

'Actually, I'm having a relationship, not an affair, and I'm having it with Paul Peschisolido.' Thank you very much, I thought.

And Jack said, 'Oh, I really like him. I thought it was an Aston Villa player.' And that was the end of that!

So while people thought the media attention on my relationship must have been a problem for me, it wasn't. It was a perceived problem, not a real problem, and I think that happens quite a lot in life. I knew I wasn't doing anything wrong, so what did I have to worry about? You can make something into a problem, or you can choose not to let it be a problem at all. You can allow things to get you down or you can choose not to. I chose not to worry about it.

After all, when you're in the public eye, you have to realise that you can't control what people say about you. Sometimes you just have to accept that the media create a perfect storm around you. Because I'm a woman in football, that happens to me a lot. What's really important is how you deal with it.

That time the perfect storm was this young, glamorous, out-there female football executive who was sleeping with a footballer. That was what people wanted to see – so that was the story the media wanted to tell, whether it was the whole truth or not. Of course, it's not nice to be the person in the middle of that story and I can understand how people want to put the duvet over their head and hope it all goes away. And, in fact, the most sensible thing to do is just to ignore it until it really does go away. You have to remember that no one reading a paper will care about what is massive to you. People just flick through the pages and then they're tomorrow's fish-and-chip paper.

Of course, that sort of situation can become uncomfortable. When I was 19, I was sent on a training course by LBC. There, one of the lecturers warned us, 'Rumour equals reputation.' At the time I thought, What the hell does that mean? What are you talking about? But it's true. If a rumour circulates that you can't manage a certain problem, does that mean you can't manage a crisis? Does that mean you're not managing your business? That you can't make a decision? The rumour will eventually impact on your reputation, whether it's true or not.

But as for the attention on Paul and me, things eased after he was transferred to Stoke City – a move that really had nothing to do with the interest in our relationship. In fact, I liked it when he played for me because I got to watch my team and my boyfriend at the same time. It's exciting watching your other half play football, really lovely. And Paul's a good player. In the end, he came back to play for Birmingham again, then moved on to West Bromwich Albion, which means I've sold my husband twice, and made a good profit both times. Not many women can say that!

All in all, for me, falling in love at work was far from the car crash it could have been. And, nowadays, as a boss, I don't object to people having relationships within the organisation – after all, I'm hardly one to criticise! I find it unrealistic that companies ban relationships between staff: most couples meet in the office, because that is where they spend most of their time.

But that doesn't mean you get carte blanche to do whatever you like. I don't have hard and fast rules but, generally, one relationship is fine; more than one is not. You can't treat the office like singles night at your local. It's wise to think seriously before you start a relationship in the office. As I say, it didn't affect me, but it might have affected Paul. He never really said anything so I don't know for sure, but I'd guess he was a bit less one of the lads and didn't fit in quite so much.

Ultimately, the potential fallout comes down your reputa-tion. Are you having a fling or a relationship? In terms of repu-tation, the first is very different from the second. Also, if you've had a fling with someone in your office and then you fall out, would you still be able to work with him or her? It might be awkward or embarrassing. I'd imagine the office might suddenly become a depressing place to go. What if you had a fling and they liked you more than you liked them? That has the potential to become unpleasant too.

So if you do like someone at work, weigh up the effect a relationship with them might have on your work life and decide whether it's worth risking. If my board had said to me, 'Either you finish with Paul or you leave,' I would have left – a pretty good sign that the relationship was worth pursuing.

You have to use your judgement. There's a huge difference between having it off on the photocopier at the Christmas party and starting a serious relationship that you know is going somewhere. So, if you do just want to sleep with someone, I'd just say, make sure they're from a rival firm and then you can find out what they're up to at the same time!

What I really condemn is relationships between a married boss and someone who works in the same organisation. It puts everyone in a very awkward position and seriously undermines the boss's reputation. If you're having affairs, treating your partner badly, not seeing your kids, who will believe you when you say, 'I'm a professional, upright person?' And these things usually become known to everyone in the office. When you have a position of responsibility, and particularly when you're in the public eye, you have to take that responsibility seriously.

But back to Paul and me. There's a massive difference between starting a relationship and keeping it together over months, years and decades. Crucially, we make a good team. I spoke recently to a successful woman who had just split up with her husband, and the fundamental problem was that they were both fiercely ambitious. I believe this is a common cause of marriage breakdowns: when two people are fighting to get ahead in their careers, it's family life that slips through the net.

A good relationship works because – and there is only one reason – your common goal is the security of your family, whether you have a huge rabble of kids or it's just the two of you and a budgie. For example, I have just found out that tonight I've got to fly off for an unplanned meeting. My daughter is in the middle of exams and I was expecting to go home to Birmingham tonight to see her, but now I can't. I have to say to Paul, 'I've got to go and do what I've got to go and do. I can't cancel,' and I know he will cancel what he's doing and take over.

Next week he'll have a match on a Saturday and, of course, as a manager he cannot fail to be there, so I'll have to cancel whatever I'm doing. It's about understanding the pressure each other is under, and prioritising what is most important. Neither of us would ever say, 'I'm going out for a drink with a friend, so I can't do it.' The truth is that something has to give.

A lot of people believe that women can have it all, mainly because the press identify some women as perfect wives, mothers, employees or bosses, stylish, sophisticated and successful – but Superwoman is a myth. No woman can do it all; no woman I have ever met believes that they *do* do it all.

Working women, no matter what they do, understand they can only do what they can do; no more and no less. Paul and I make our life work by understanding our priorities – which mostly translates into having the self-discipline to say no. No, we will not go to the many parties we are invited to. No, we will not attend many functions or fun events we are invited to. No, we will not palm the kids off and go away on our own, and no, we never put the children in the kids' club on holiday. You will never see us falling out of a pub or nightclub (God forbid) drunk.

And the reason we say no is that we know what's important to us: our two children. They want and need us more than any job or career does. Then, between our work and our kids, there's each other.

Now, with two teenage children, we have worked out how to run our lives in the smoothest way possible. If I call him it's because I need to speak to him urgently and vice versa. We never call during the day for a chat, as I'm always too busy and he's always too distracted. My PA sends him a copy of my schedule every week and he compares it with what he has to do. I change it to suit him, as my work and meetings are normally more flexible than his. I can't ask him to move a fixture to a Thursday to suit my bank meeting! At the moment, I am trying to spend only two nights a week – when I'm not filming – away from home, Tuesday and Wednesday, which means I can do three full days in London and go back to watch most of our West Ham matches, my son's own fixture list allowing!

Some people say that I'm not supportive of Paul, as I can't remember the last time I saw his team play and I don't attend his club functions with him. It's not because I don't want to, it's because I don't have time. When he's out, I'm at home with the kids. At weekends our children have a million things to do, which are their priorities, and because I'm their mother, they're mine too.

Paul understands – and, judging by past experience, he's never been too fussed whether I come to watch or not! I remember once, when he was playing for Sheffield, I asked him to get some tickets so the children and I could come and see him. I turned up with the kids in a posh coat – it was in the middle of winter – picked up the tickets and set off to the directors' area to be told: 'Oh, no, not that way, just go down there.' So I went the way they had shown me and came to a turnstile – I hadn't gone through one for 15 years. After that, if we went to see Paul play, I organised my own tickets!

It is tough to juggle everything. It takes an awful lot of dedication to make a career, a relationship and family life work, and you have to focus on what is important. Your individual focus is on your career but together your focus is on your family, and we just have to keep making sure we don't let anything slip.

It must be so difficult for two very ambitious people to bring up a family, if neither is prepared to give an inch. It's hard enough for me and Paul, and family life has always been a priority for us both. We've had different cycles in our careers, and have taken turns to be the one to focus more on the family.

I think for it to work one of you will always take a greater share of responsibility for the children, and Paul and I have both been that person at different times.

When the children were young, I took that role. Running Birmingham City was, of course, a big and demanding job, but it wasn't a global business that involved huge amounts of travel. It meant I could take the children to school in the morning and be back home at a reasonable hour. Meanwhile Paul was a professional footballer with a career that would take him away for six weeks at a time to Central and South America. He played for Canada so he'd often be over there, away for the summer working on the Concacaf Cup, a major tournament. Then he was moved to Stoke, he was moved to Sheffield, he was moved to Fulham, and all the time we, as a family unit, stayed in Birmingham. I was the one who was there, keeping the family running.

Then it switched. As Paul's career as a player was coming to an end, my career in business was really taking off, so he was able to spend more time at home, ferrying the children around, while I could put in longer hours and travel more. The balance still changes all the time. At the moment, Paul is moving into management, so he needs more time for that, and I'm hoping to be able to slow down a bit. These cycles work well for us and it would be nice if the pattern continued.

It does mean that there can be a big difference in what each of us is earning at any particular time, and I know for some couples this can cause problems, but money and the question of who earns more has never been an issue with us. When we first met, Paul earned a lot more than I did, even though I was running the club – that's how football salaries work – and the balance has swung back and forth over the years.

Whether or not you can cope with this is all to do with the way you think about your money. Paul and I see it as our money, not his money and my money, and we have one bank account. We both do as we like with it. I'd never say to him, 'How much have you spent on that?' and he would never question how much I was spending. I believe in equality in marriage in the sense that you are like one person. So it is *our* money, our house, our car, our life.

When you have a situation where the person who earns less feels inadequate, it's not really about the money but about how each person's contribution to the relationship is treated. If a high-earning man drives around in a Maserati and his wife in a beaten-up Mini, the message she gets is: 'I can afford this for me but not for you.' In that marriage, money expresses the pecking order. I wouldn't want to be in a relationship with someone who wasn't an equal partner, and I wouldn't have married anyone I didn't respect enough to be my equal partner.

It's all about appreciating the other's contribution. I couldn't be at West Ham for an hour if it wasn't for Paul being at home in Birmingham, and he couldn't have played at Fulham, if I hadn't been in Birmingham, looking after the kids. Frankly, the person who stays at home probably deserves the Maserati, because they do the menial stuff that no one credits, and which is never considered award-winning work. The kids hate you because you're at home and you're the disciplinarian, saying, 'No, you can't do that.' Then your partner comes in and says, 'Of course you can,' because they haven't spent the whole day having their ear chewed off about whatever it is!

That said, while for some years marriage is all about your family, as our children get older, our relationship is moving into a new phase. Recently Paul was in London for the night without the children, for dinner and a football-club do. In the morning, before he went home to Birmingham and I came to work, we went out for breakfast, and for the first time in my life I could see ahead to our retirement. It's not on my mind very often – I'm only 42 – but that day I could see a time when Paul and I would be together, on our own, without the kids, enjoying each other's company. And I think it would be very nice to live in London, where there are plenty of things to do, plenty of places to eat, plenty of places to pootle around and where our kids can come and see us.

I'm looking forward to it.

CH.7
LEARNING TO LEAD

Fortunately for me, all the juggling and balancing and schedule-tweaking my life demands plays to one of my strengths – leadership. People often think of great leaders as charismatic, rallying-the-troops, Winston Churchill-type figures. To me, that's only partly true, as it misses out a massive chunk of what it means to really lead people.

Great leadership is as much about paying attention to the nitty-gritty as it is about sounding the part. As well as the purple prose, you need someone who makes sure that 'for the want of a nail' the kingdom isn't lost, as the old saying goes. Both of these leadership styles have their place, of course. And you do find that the classic chairman/chief-executive partnership heading up a strong business often provides a combination of the two.

So, the face of the company will be the statesmanlike, charismatic chairman, with a chief executive behind them who can roll up their sleeves and do the work. The classic example of this for me is Terry Leahy who, as chief exec, ran Tesco so successfully for years. He is one of the least showy people you will ever meet, but I remember him saying, 'All my ambitions are for Tesco,' and when he said it you believed it. He was an actions-speak-louder-than-words leader. Steely and driven, but never flash.

It takes time to build your own operational style, through your conscious decisions to do things a certain way. When I was younger I simply wanted to win at everything I did, but as you get more mature you learn the art of taking people with you on your journey. You begin to understand the importance of building trust and spirit within an organisation and the importance of standing for something, and making that *something* important.

At the start of my career, my primary inspiration for great leadership came in the form of David Sullivan. When I first met him, I was instantly struck by what an incredibly impressive person he is. He had a very clear vision of what he was doing and how he wanted to do it. When you are 19 you rarely meet people with such clarity. Plus, he was interested in my views and what I believed in, and as a young person that is equally important: not many people want to know what you think. Having worked at Saatchi's and LBC, I wanted a change, and the idea of being someone's right-hand person was very attractive.

It was a good decision. David is very well educated, very bright and knowledgeable on pretty much any subject. He's a deep thinker. He is also very logical and has the ability to cut through to what is important. We are on the same wavelength, which means I can say one word and he gets my train of thought straight away and vice versa. We don't agree on everything but we do respect each others opinion.

David has instilled in me a can-do attitude and the importance of having enormous energy and, perhaps most importantly he has taught me to understand the value of persistence and perseverance. I remember, in the days before email, I used to get 100-page faxes from him almost every day. Now it's emails – morning, noon and night. Very often he will email me at one in the morning, I'll reply, and he'll say, 'You should be asleep,' then I'll respond, 'So should you.'

He and I found ourselves naturally slotting into a classic chairman/chief-executive working relationship in the early days, him with the vision and me with the ability to get my hands dirty and turn all the ideas into reality. What we achieved at Birmingham shows just how well our skills combined. Together we really did rewrite the way football clubs were run, and the things we introduced there have been copied across the industry.

As I have got older I have developed my own style and way of doing things, and along the way I have met many other great leaders. They may run world-class companies, small family businesses, or may even be one-man-band operations, but they share the same traits. They are able to communicate a long-term strategy, as well as short-term goals. They believe in life-long learning, can listen to others and show integrity. And, crucially, they have the ability to take people's hearts on a journey.

Achieving that, for me, is about respecting people and imparting passion and enthusiasm to them. Enthusiasm rubs off from one person to another, so you need to be fundamentally positive about your organisation. You need to give people a sense of purpose, the confidence that there is a role for them. And then you have to monitor them and give them useful feedback. That means meeting them regularly and saying, 'Over the past month, these are the things you have done well and these are the things you have not done so well. This is how I would like you to do them. This is how you can improve them.' The best thing you can give your workers when you're a business leader is your time.

That doesn't mean having to be unfailingly positive, even when you are not happy with someone's performance. Everyone who works for me knows that my expectations are high. My HR director will say to people, 'There is no hiding place in Karren's organisations. If you want a little job where you can hide away, don't come and work here, but if you have ambition and she spots something in you she'll push you to achieve more.'

And so I like to create a creative and happy atmosphere, but with a focus on hard work. I know I have to leave my family behind to work late, so I understand the sacrifices everyone else is making and want to make the process as enjoyable as possible. Often when we work through the night, my team and I will have different food deliveries, put the football on in the background and have duvets and makeshift beds brought in to make an adult crèche for those who need a nap.

No joke, but very often people are sad when the hard work is over and the solution is delivered: the fun of the challenge has given everyone a lift. Everyone knows they have been part of a good team to overcome a problem and provide a solution that has made the company better. It is about a dedication to the job, a willingness to do whatever it takes to resolve the problem – which is quite the opposite of doing whatever you can in the time you can make available to it.

To this end, getting everyone involved in finding a solution is vital. That's why I have introduced cost committees in my organisations, authorised to go into any part of the organisation and look at where money is being spent. Their job is to save money and they would receive a bonus as a percentage of the money they saved – quite an incentive! So, if we bought air-conditioning and the supplier said they had put in five units, they would be up in the rafters to check that there were really five units. Very often they would find there were four. The cost committee would have the authority to question any expenditure, which meant that everyone had to think about what they were spending. It was all about drilling home the message that looking after the company's money is important and we have to work together to be successful: we have to work very hard for the company and not incur any costs that we can't afford.

That said, it's absolutely essential that communication goes two ways. The most impressive business leaders are not those who can only drive home *their* point of view or make *their* strategy happen – although those things are important. They are the people who can sit in a room, listen to everybody's opinion, then work out which is the one to follow, or which parts to put together into a strategy that can be delivered. Angela Ahrendts at Burberry is world class at doing this. And it's something I have always been able to do. Listen, understand, adopt and implement.

In contrast, the steamrolling personality who says, 'No, we're going to do it this way,' is very easily stressed and makes others stressed too. That type of person is not used to challenge, to being asked, 'Why are we doing this?', 'Why aren't we doing that?', 'What's important?' and 'Does this match our core values?' And they will be asked these things, however high up the ladder they climb. But instead of being able to articulate any of these points, they lose it and swear.

That's not my style. I try to run a flat-line hierarchy, as far as I can. I don't like creating complicated organisational structures – we're all there to do one thing: make our business better. It doesn't matter whether you're here or there, we're all involved.

But if I've got an issue with one member of the team, it has to be shared with everybody. I will bring everyone in and say, 'This has happened, this is how I intend to deal with it, and this is why it's important that we do this, this and this.' When certain people have made a mistake, they find that difficult. But I also believe in ownership. If you don't know who owns the problem, you don't know how to find the solution.

People often expect the person in charge to have all the answers when a problem arises, but great leadership is not about what you know how to do. It's about how you behave when you don't – immediately – know what to do. How do you cope? What do you do next?

The most important thing is to work out *why* you don't know what to do. And then start from the other end: look at who can do what. Who can help you? Go and ask other people for guidance and listen to them. Then rely on your core values and trust yourself.

What I have learnt is that the best way to approach a problem is to break it down and flip everything the other way round. Instead of focusing on the issue at hand – here I am and I don't know what I'm going to do – I consider where I want to be and how I'm going to get there. Set the marker and work backwards, rather than trying to think your way out of the situation

1. Nanny Rose, my father's mother, one of the strong women in my family who have had such an influence on me. A real grafter, she worked until she was nearly 80. **2.** Me as a two-year-old (what a bonnet!) with my brother Darren and our other grandmother, Nanny Nina, in Cattolica in Italy, her homeland. Nanny Nina was the feistiest character I've ever known, but also the most loving and generous woman.

3. With Nanny Nina and Darren again, playing dress-up as a four-year-old in our garden in Mitchell Road, Edmonton. I was always the queen and my brother the villain. Starting as I meant to go on. **4.** On a rare escape from convent school. My friend Charlotte Peeling (as she was then) and I, aged 16, at a party. Nice hair! Well, it was 1985.

5. Arriving at Birmingham City Football Club in 1993, aged 23. I'm standing in front of my pride and joy – my pale blue Porsche. **6.** A fantastic evening in May 1999, when my husband Paul's team Fulham were promoted and he was Player of the Year. Kevin Keegan, his manager, and the owner Mohamed Al-Fayed threw a massive party at the top of Harrods. I would have been 30. **7.** A year into my time at Birmingham City FC and I'm in the dressing room with some of the players – probably the first and last time I went in there!

8. June 10th 1995, my wedding day: Paul and I at the Dorchester Hotel in London. 17 years on and two children later, and we're still happy. **9.** Not too many pre-wedding jitters. Having a cup of tea with my dad at my parents' house Owls Hall, waiting to get my dress on and get to the church.

10. My daughter Sophia and I at our mother and toddler group, in 1997. Everyone in the family calls her Dolly, and you can see why – she is such a doll here.
11. At Paul's family's farm in Italy, in 1998, on a holiday with a few of the in-laws – who are all lovely. I'm at the front right with Sophia on my knee.

11

12. September 5th 1999, my son Paolo's first birthday party. I can't say I made that cake, but there is a bond between the two of us that can never be broken. **13.** A very young Sophia and I at the safari park in the Midlands on a family day out in 1997. I look at that picture and feel such a strong bond of love. My kids are my life. **14.** On a trip to France in 2004 with my Birmingham City board – and Paul. That made it a rare and rather glamorous weekend for us without the children. **15.** Christmas 2007 with my mother, her parents Nanny Nina and Granddad Gerald, and Sophia and Paolo. I cannot remember a Christmas without my mum and dad by my side.

16. My mum, dad and I at my colleague and friend David Sullivan's 60th birthday party at The Dorchester in February 2010. Paul Anchor, the singer, was the entertainment.
17. With my West Ham chairman David Gold, a real gentleman and a true friend, in 2008.

18. A happy moment for David Gold, me and David Sullivan on February 11th, 2011, just after West Ham had been announced as the preferred bidders for the Olympic Stadium. Little did we know that a few months later they would take away the keys! **19.** David Cameron and me in Birmingham in March 2007. I'm a Tory and I'd love to work with the Government on the issue of women and business.

LEADERS IN LONDON

Principal Sponsor:

CSC

LEADERS IN LONDON

Principal Sponsor:

CSC

20. At Buckingham Palace in 2007 with the Duchess of Cornwall and Jacqueline Gold, chief executive of Ann Summers. This was my second visit to the Palace, for a reception recognising successful businesswomen.

21. Speaking at the Leaders in London International Leadership Summit in November 2007, addressing the serious issue of getting more women into the boardroom. With me on the platform are City 'superwoman' Nicola Horlick and businesswoman Sally Preston.

22

THE **APPRENTICE**

WEDNESDAY, OCTOBER, 9PM ON BBC ONE

23

24

22. With Lord Sugar and Nick Hewer at the launch of *The Apprentice* in 2010. I had come from selling cheese on a freezing market stall, as we were filming at the time. I was totally knackered and look it. Who said telly was glamorous! **23.** Nick Hewer and I in 2011, having just appeared on *Daybreak* to promote the new series of *The Apprentice*. Nick is a great person, a good friend and total star on *Countdown*. We always have lots of fun together. **24.** At the National Television Awards 2012 in an Alessandra Rich gown – my favourite dress. *The Apprentice* was nominated for best reality programme. We lost to *I'm A Celebrity Get Me Out Of Here!* Oh well, it could have been worse, we could have lost to *Come Dine With Me!*

you feel stuck in. And from that you will create a clear path that everybody can follow.

My experiences at West Ham, particularly our bid for the Olympic Stadium, make the perfect case in point. I have had to deploy all my leadership skills to start to turn that club around. When I arrived at there as vice-chairman in January 2010, even the offices were horrible, painted a dirty green with a grubby burgundy carpet. There were no windows, everyone had a tiny single cubbyhole to work in, and it was just awful. I couldn't motivate myself in that environment, let alone other people.

Typically for me, the job was something that I had decided on very quickly. I would go in, turn things around and move on – just as I had thought at Birmingham, where I ended up staying 16 years! I should have known. As it turned out, the surface grottiness would be the least of the problems I had to tackle at West Ham.

Since I started in football, I have seen it become a far less male-dominated environment. There is much more acceptance nowadays that football is something that you can enjoy if you are a woman. Funnily enough, I think the glamour now associated with footballers and their WAGs has played a part in that change, as well as the wider shifts that have taken place in society and people's attitudes. But regardless of what's behind it, there's no doubt things have changed a lot for football in the 20 years I have been involved.

That's why it was such a shock when I arrived at West Ham and all I found was the same old male domination. It was like entering a time warp: the club was still all about fast cars and sharp suits and 'birds' and going out on a Friday night. There was no ethos of: we are here to work professionally and honestly and we have a responsibility to do that. It was all about: What's in it for me?

Here was an organisation that was £100 million in debt and yet it was still running up hundreds of thousands of pounds worth of taxi bills alone. The chief executive had a company Aston Martin and he spent £30,000 on his company credit card in several months. You could see where the problems stemmed from – if the boss doesn't care enough to worry about every penny, why should anybody else?

Things had to change. When I first came to West Ham, there was only one really decent hotel in the area – the Four Seasons – but I refused to stay there because I couldn't justify rolling in from that place each morning. I felt it would send people the message: you might lose your job as we have to cut our expenditure dramatically, but thanks very much I'm off to my £300-a-night hotel. That is just not me.

There were no expectations of anybody. I called it the West Ham country club, because everyone could do what they liked: come in when they liked, go when they liked. It wasn't a serious environment where you knew what was expected of you, where you knew what you could become, how you could be promoted, what you could achieve if you worked hard and made an effort, in terms of bonus and career prospects. And who wants to really graft in an environment that does not offer the opportunity to have a serious career?

Meanwhile people were making the most appalling decisions. Managers would put a £2 million deal on the books and be chuffed with it, and I would look at it and say, 'Yes, but in return for bringing in the £2 million of business, you've committed to spend £2.5 million with that company. That is not a good deal – it is a terrible, terrible, terrible deal.' And they'd go, 'Oh yeah …' and the penny would drop. When it didn't, they didn't have a future with West Ham.

My view was that I had to pull three levers to turn the club around, so to speak. The first was to sort out the business; the second was to create more capital – put simply, get us some money; and the third was to create a future. So I set myself three objectives: cut the costs, balance the books and deliver the Olympic Stadium – a new home for the club. And in my first year the club made a profit for the first time that anyone could remember; the debt was cut from a £100 million to £70 million by raising new money and generating more revenue; and I did deliver the Olympic Stadium.

But, after that, things didn't go quite according to plan.

The thing was, when Manchester City Council built the stadium for the 2002 Commonwealth Games, they already had a deal in place with a football club – Manchester City – to move there afterwards. That didn't happen with the Olympic Stadium and West Ham, which in my view was a big mistake.

The Olympic Stadium is right on our doorstep at the club. You can see it from the boardroom window at Upton Park, our current home. And the stadium should have been built in a way that, as a natural legacy of the Games, it would come to West Ham, and West Ham should have made that happen. That's a process that should have been initiated right at the start of the project. But it wasn't and, having arrived at West Ham with the Olympic Stadium almost finished, I wanted to deliver it to the club and the community – somehow.

Moving would make a big difference for the club, I knew. The Olympic Stadium is twice the size in capacity, and of course the more seats you have the more money you can generate, since you can entertain more people. There were other benefits, too. Upton Park is in the middle of a housing estate, so traffic is quite an issue, whereas at the Olympic Stadium there are seven interconnecting rail lines. Plus, of course, there is so much opportunity just tied to being in a brand-spanking-new stadium. It helps bring the crowds in and it changes the face of the brand.

At first, I thought it would be a relatively easy process since it seemed we were the only viable contender. The stadium is in our borough, and we had all sorts of plans, which were in keeping with the ethos of the Games, to open the facility to the community. We started to negotiate with the Olympic Park Legacy Company (OPLC), which is responsible for the long-term future of the Olympic Park and its facilities, and everything seemed to be on track. Then, on the day that we handed in our application to Downing Street, our rivals Tottenham Hotspur put in an application.

It is a free country, and of course anyone could go for it, but the fact that Daniel Levy, the chairman of Tottenham, didn't have the balls to call me to say that they had decided to bid really annoyed me, because we were friends. All's fair in love and war, is my attitude, so what was I going to say? 'You are not allowed?' Not at all, but I would have appreciated him being straightforward about it. I can't stand that sort of sneaky approach – I am a direct person and it is just not my style. I would far rather get something out in the open.

Spurs entering the process at the eleventh hour came as a big surprise. While I knew there would be other bidders for the stadium, I didn't think that there would be another football club. It was almost impossible to think then – and still is now – that a north London club would move miles across the city to east London and still want to call itself Tottenham.

Their logic was flawed, in my view. The Olympic Park Legacy Company is called that for a reason, yet Tottenham viewed the whole thing as a simple land deal. Their plan was to bulldoze the stadium – and bollocks to everybody who has put the money in, including the taxpayer – to create a new football stadium. It was: we are a rich football club, we will use it for football and no one else is going to get a look in. And I think that sort of heavy-handed approach is why many people in football don't have many friends. The stadium should be a landmark, a reminder of this great moment in London's history, like the Bird's Nest Stadium built in Beijing for the 2008 Olympics. As a tourist you would go and visit that, but you wouldn't if they bulldozed it and built some football stadium in its place.

Tottenham coming into the running changed the whole tone of the competition and really soured it for me, I won't lie. I thought it was a real shame that the issue of the Olympic legacy was being turned into a football debate. It should never have been Tottenham versus West Ham – we just didn't approach it in that sort of short-sighted way; we had our eye on the far bigger picture.

But we had to face facts. Suddenly we had a very fierce, very rich competitor, who had far greater resources than we did. Spurs had been working on a stadium project for several years, so they had already employed a team of specialists – architects, designers, lawyers – whereas up until that point our bid was principally handled by me and just one other person from West Ham. The two of us would turn up to the OPLC to discuss the bid and Spurs would have a whole team there, all experts in their field.

We didn't have the money to employ architects, designers and lawyers to compete with Spurs head on – we just weren't in a position to throw a million pounds at it. But we needed that level of expertise if we were to stand a chance of winning. It was clear that we had gone from leader of the pack to very much the second horse in the race.

Right, I thought. If we didn't pull together a similar team of experts, we wouldn't win. We had to match Spurs man for man. My job was to find people who could deliver – and I had the added problem that we didn't have any money to pay them.

So this was how my thinking went: what is the end game? The end game is that we get the stadium. Then we've got to convert it into a multi-purpose, world-class stadium. The builders who would win the contract to convert it would get more than £95 million from West Ham and the OPLC. So I considered who I wanted to work with; who would do so on a contingency basis; who would be prepared to put up the resources, put up the design, put up the architect, and do all of that on the basis that if we won they'd get the work. Then I had to sell that deal to another organisation, the London Borough of Newham, and I went to the retail property group Westfield, who had already made a huge impact in East London through the development of the Westfield Shopping centre in Stratford.

Then I had to do the same to get a lawyer. It was all about having to adapt and work backwards: this was what we were going to end up with, so we'd work back from there.

And we did it. We were awarded the stadium in 2011, a fantastic result. We were so pleased – I was so pleased. I knew we would create something that lived up to what everybody said the site could be: a sporting legacy that the world would envy. For me, this was an opportunity to do something historic.

But then Spurs and another club, Leyton Orient, who also threw their hat into the ring, challenged the decision in the courts and, as a result of an anonymous complaint to Europe, the Government changed the process. We had been going to put in £60 million, and the OPLC was expected to put in £35m – but it was suggested to the European Commission that this breached state aid rules. The complaint could have tied the stadium up in legal knots for many years, threatening the 2017 World Athletics Championship, which was going to be held there.

So the whole bidding process was withdrawn – as was our preferred-bidder status. Our hard-fought victory had been taken away from us. That was two years of really hard graft, a few hundred thousand pounds had been spent and we had nothing to show for it. Having being handed the keys to the stadium, they had decided to change the locks.

It was a real blow. I felt depressed that forces outside my control had effectively collapsed a very competitive process and was sure that no good at all would come from it. We had been prevented from entering the stadium, but so had everyone else. It felt petty and mean-spirited to me. The attitude of some of the other interested parties appeared to be: we'll stop you having it, and anyone else, just because we want to. There was no thought to the jobs we could create, no concern for the young people in East London who would enjoy the stadium and no thought to the fact that tens of millions of pounds needed to be found to convert the stadium for future use.

The first job for me was to pick everyone up off the floor. Yes, it felt like two years had gone down the drain, but I've never met a successful person who is not determined. It's the key to my own success. I am often better under real pressure, and when all seems lost I can still dig deep enough to find a solution, can work hard to get back up again. The stadium was still there and its future could still involve West Ham. The question now was: what would we have to do to make it happen again?

As I write, the stadium is being re-tendered. This time around, we can apply to be a tenant in a converted stadium, not its owner. But as a tenant with a 99-year lease, with the facilities we need and with control over our environment, the deal could offer the same attractions, may even be better. And the one thing you'll find out about me in this process is that I see things through to the end, wherever that may take me. I'll never back down; I'll not stop fighting if I believe in something.

That stadium was ours, and that should count for something. My team and I will fight on, we'll be dogged to the end and we will let nothing or no one stand in our way, because it is right that we have it. We have to go back to the drawing board, yes, but I would pitch myself and my team against anyone. We may not have the most money, but we have the vision and the passion to deliver results and will stake our reputations on doing so, and that in my book counts for a whole lot more than a chequebook. We'll have to wait and see what the tender offers as I want to win, but not at any cost. If it's right for West Ham, then we'll bid again.

Meanwhile, we may have had a crisis on our hands, but everything else does not grind to a halt. A lot of my time in 2011 was taken up with reading legal papers and fighting the stadium battle. But then in May that year another drama unfolded, as West Ham was relegated from the Premier League. Relegation is the worst thing that can happen to a club, it really is. And of course it is an issue for everybody, but the truth is that, when it happens, the lives of the footballers and the football managers don't really change. However, it impacts on us on the business side hugely. Our job gets much harder.

We are the team behind the team that has to put it all right. But morale nosedives not only among the supporters, but among the board and the staff too. On the Monday after we were relegated, we had to be back in there for another working day and, again, it was my job to pick everybody up. I believe in being straight and told them all: 'We have got a really hard task, and we will all find out something about ourselves this year as we carve our way out of it.'

The problem is that relegation impacts on how much you can earn for the club, how many bills you can pay, what you can deliver for your shareholders. Revenue falls as the money you get from broadcast rights is much lower in the Championship; likewise, with sponsorship deals. It's the perfect example of a situation where it is really important that, rather than having a football supporter running the club, who can't get over the knock of getting relegated, you have somebody who says, 'Look, this is a business problem that requires a solution, and we have got to get busy to resolve the problem.'

What was most difficult for me was the reaction of the media, who seemed to hold me responsible. It was that confusion again, between my role and the role of the manager. I don't wear a tracksuit, I don't pick the players and I don't pick the manager, well, not on this occasion. I didn't select Avram Grant and it's public knowledge that I didn't think he was right for the role and that I felt he should be replaced. I don't go into the dressing room and tell the players how to play. I wear a suit and I run the business, and the business is the only thing I can control. And despite the fact that we finished bottom of the league in 2011, as I write I know we'll probably make over £6 million trading profit. Judge me on that rather than our league position. I left Birmingham in a blaze of glory, having sold the club for £82 million, but the things I did in that first year at West Ham are probably as impressive as my entire last few years at Birmingham.

It sometimes feels as though all my successes at West Ham have been eclipsed by the relegation, instead of observers saying, 'Thank God there are people here, despite relegation, who are running the business, changing things, doing things for the better.' But I know that I can pride myself on what I have achieved at West Ham, be it cutting costs, generating business, changing the understanding there, getting the best out of people, or winning the Olympic Stadium, which is a fantastic achievement, frankly – even if we still have many hurdles to overcome.

It's a lesson that we all need to remember in business, and in life: don't rely on other people to acknowledge your triumphs, in any situation. Have faith in yourself. I do, and I'll fight on.

Luckily, I enjoy a huge challenge! I am not easily stressed and that's a very important part of leadership. I'm at my best under pressure and I enjoy multi-tasking – in fact, the busier I am, the happier I am. My theory is that I cope well with stress partly because I have very low blood pressure. A TV make-up artist I was working with once pointed out the connection to me. We had spent a busy day moving from event to event, and at the end she asked me, 'Do you have low blood pressure?' When I nodded, she said, 'I thought so. You remained calm under so much pressure – being put on the spot over and over and over again.' She might have a point, I thought.

Then again, 'stress' is a dangerous word because it doesn't really mean anything. You may be annoyed, you may be disappointed, but is that being 'stressed?' I've seen people who cannot cope with challenge. I've seen people who cannot cope when others aren't listening to them – eventually, they explode. That's about not having the mental capacity to deal with what is happening when things seem to be going out of control. When you are under pressure, your true operational style is revealed. How you cope is the real measure of what type of leader you are.

When you're a leader, dealing with stress is not about 'chilling out', whatever that means. It's about having the ability to stop and listen. If you're very stressed, it's because you haven't communicated what you want to happen and people are not doing what you want done – either because they don't understand what you want to achieve, or they don't believe in it. It is all about winning their heads and their hearts.

If I do ever get stressed, it's because of incompetence. Employees who think they're better than they are are a real danger within an organisation. My solution is simple: I try always to employ very competent people. It's said that if you employ people who are better than you are, you prove that you are better than them, and I really believe that. I always employ the best people I can find and hope they are better than me.

Of course, things still go wrong on occasion, and if someone makes a serious error, I can be very direct. People are under no illusions as to whether I'm happy or not with their performance. I think the most-feared word in my organisation, spoken by me, would be 'disappointed'. If I say, 'I'm really disappointed in you,' you know you've hit rock bottom.

Now, I can't talk about leadership without addressing what some people might see as the elephant in the room: that I'm a woman who's in charge. There is a lot of stuff said about female bosses, and a lot of it is rubbish. Of course there are differences between male and female leaders – and I don't see any need to erase them.

In the 1980s when I was at starting out in the working world, the senior women were always running around in big shoulder pads, screaming at the top of their voices and bullying people in that greed-is-good Gordon Gekko style. All because they thought they should be like men. The more ballsy they seemed, the more seriously they would be taken – or that was the idea, at least. But bawling and bullying never equates to good management, whether a woman or a man is doing it.

The differences between men and women should be celebrated, I believe. We are different, so we're bound to be different in our leadership styles – and it's important to remember that there is no blueprint for great leadership.

In my experience, women are natural nurturers: they want to see people grow and develop. They like working in a team and getting the best out of their staff, and they understand the old maxim that 'No man (or woman) should be left behind.' Above all, I believe that women tend to do what's right, when it's right, regardless of their own self-interest.

Male leaders are almost always more political in the way that they operate: looking at the bigger picture, keeping an eye out for what job to apply for next. The motto of some that I have known and worked with sometimes seems to be self-interest above the interests of their team or their company.

Men are far less emotional and they can see the bottom line quickly, traits which have their uses, but they are less able, in my opinion, to find the best person to do the job, as they always go for the obvious. Women will take a chance on someone, and help them to explore their talents – which means they will often enjoy far more loyalty from their teams.

Of course, I am often asked how I achieved it, working as a leader in such a male-dominated environment as football. To be honest, I often think the better question is why. Well, I saw a business opportunity and I was not scared to go after it. I saw football as a brand, saw that it had the potential to be worth a fortune, saw an opportunity, since I had an understanding of business. These are the sort of opportunities that private equity – the big-money investors – always looks for: the opportunity to brand, build and develop something into something far more valuable.

Yes, it is a male-dominated world and yes, sometimes that can be difficult, but it's the way you handle yourself that is key to being a success in such industries. In that regard, I have three key pieces of advice to any woman in a similar position.

Number one: mix. Ridiculous as it may sound, lots of men are intimidated by having a woman in an office which doesn't usually have one. So the most important thing is for the men to get a measure of who you are and what you stand for. That doesn't mean trying to drink them under the table in the pub on a Friday night, then attempting to discipline them on a Monday morning. You do not want to be one of the lads, and neither are you one of the girls. You are a professional. You handle yourself well at all times You do your job consistently well and show a mature attitude. And never be afraid to promote yourself. If you don't, who is going to do it for you?

Number two: celebrate your uniqueness. I will often find myself the only woman in meetings and as a result I am often more noticed and remembered than any of the men in the room. I ensure that I speak up when I have something to say, that I maintain eye contact and that I always explain my position if it is not in agreement with that of the other people at the meeting. I am confident in my values and my opinions and therefore I have the confidence to speak when I want to. And just because I work with men does not mean that I dress like one!

Number three: handle the difficult men with class. It's important to be decisive and shut down a problem effectively and quickly. You must stand up for yourself and show that you cannot and will not be intimidated. I find that speaking to someone in front of their colleagues in the right tone, followed by a private word, shows that you can handle yourself in a mature way. It also acts as a warning to everyone, not just the offender. Then, once you've acted, don't mention the situation again. It shows that you've got clear boundaries but that you want to work with your male colleagues, not against them.

And you have to remember that there may well be pros and cons tied to having a man or a woman running the show. But, ultimately, the ability – or inability – to lead will come from an individual's strengths and weaknesses, not their gender.

After all, stereotypes can only take you so far. The person who taught me a great lesson about navigating emotional situations at work was, in fact, a man. Roger Bannister is a different sort of leader again, who has been very important in my working life. As my financial director at Birmingham City, he was an enormous asset to me, as a very calm and very constant presence when I was young and still growing up.

You might assume it would be me, because I was the woman in charge, but it was Roger who would say, 'I think so-and-so is under the weather,' or 'This person's not very happy,' or 'That one's got a problem.' Because I was – am – so busy, sometimes I didn't see what was at the end of my nose. He taught me the importance of actively looking at what is going on, keeping an eye out for any budding problems, in addition to listening when people bring their concerns to you. As well as that, he showed me the importance not only of motivating the team in the workplace but of looking out for them outside the office, too.

I would say to him, 'What's wrong with X?', and he would reply, 'Well, his marriage is breaking up. Didn't you know?', and no, I wouldn't have noticed. In the early days of my career, I came to work free of emotional burdens and presumed everyone else did, too. My view was that you come to work, you do your job, you go home.

If we had interviewed someone who was particularly nervous for a job, I would say, 'What on earth is there to be nervous about?' Roger would reply, 'Well, don't you understand?' And I didn't understand at all: to me an interview was an opportunity to show off what you could do. What I learnt from Roger was to be more sympathetic, to realise that, if it's important to that person, then it's important – even if it wouldn't affect me. As a leader, you need to be patient and tolerant.

Not everybody has the ability to be unemotional, and that was a valuable lesson: as a leader you have to ensure that people are in a workplace that helps them, listens and cares – as well as rewarding them. That makes for a fantastic, thriving working environment. As an employee, if you work at a place you can trust and believe in, and where you want to stay, you are far more likely give it your all.

Of course, a question you might ask is: how do you learn to be a leader, if you are not in that sort of position already? That was one of the reasons that I got involved with Avon in a mentoring role. It's a company that believes that every woman has the right to financial independence. As it says, it puts mascara on lashes and food on tables! Avon offers economic opportunity for women, by giving them the support and the infrastructure to set up quickly and start earning immediately. Today, in more than 100 countries, around 6.5 million active, independent Avon Sales Representatives – of whom the vast majority are women – are realizing their desire to have as much, or as little financial independence as they decide.

That's the real power that sets this company apart. If you want to earn enough for a few special treats, or over £1 million a year, you can. You decide when, you decide how. Many of these women entrepreneurs would not have access to credit, or be able to set up a business overnight. But Avon operates on the basis that everyone should have the chance to support themselves and their families in a flexible way, without set hours and a set workplace. Whether in Moscow or Leeds, women can leverage this flexibility to be the head of their own business. Now that's something to be really proud of. I have met many hundreds of ladies running their Avon business who have found their own balance, fitting in their goals with their family, enjoying their financial independence and finding being in charge of their life and career hugely rewarding. And who can blame them?

For me, it's living proof that being a business leader is not about the size of the business, but about achieving whatever aim you set out for yourself. It doesn't matter if you are in charge of 1,000 people or a business that makes £1,000. In the end, motivating and leading *yourself* is the most essential step of all.

CH.8
MY CHILDREN

Learning to lead and building a career is one thing. Learning to parent is quite another – but they were two challenges I faced at the same time. Because once Paul and I were together, I wanted to get pregnant quickly, which meant having my babies as I was still climbing the ladder.

Nonetheless, my plan had always been to have children and, I hoped, in my twenties, so I would be young enough to enjoy their company when they were older. I knew that there would never be an 'ideal time' when I was working, which meant that if I waited I might put it off for ever. And it's true: many of my friends have waited for that mythical perfect moment, which, sadly for them, has never come around. As it turned out, I was 27 when I had Sophia, my eldest, and I've never looked back.

I didn't worry that children would be any sort of impediment to my career. I just thought, I'm going to have my family and I'll have to make it work. Of course it didn't turn out to be quite as simple as that, but I believe some women think about it too much, and still end up compromising their careers. Perhaps they don't take promotions, thinking that they may have children and the burden would be too much. In my experience, there is never an ideal time and worrying about when will often mean you leave it too late and miss out. If you think about things for ever, you can come up with as many reasons not to do something as to do it, so you have to just go for it.

But be under no illusions: it is very, very hard to have a career and a family. As I have said, until I met Paul the plan was that I would have children on my own so I could be in complete control – of course – but now I look back and think, Thank God I didn't do that! I take my hat off to single working mothers, I can't imagine how difficult it must be to cope on your own with the stresses of working and family.

Famously, when Sophia was born in May 1996, I took just three days off work. I had her on the Friday and I was back at work on the Monday. I regret that, but at the time I felt I had no choice. People criticise me for it, but it wasn't as though I was thinking, I know, I'll drop a couple of kids and march off to the office. Maternity-leave provision was minimal in those days and attitudes were very different. Flexible working didn't exist as it does now – I hadn't even heard of it as a concept, let alone an actual choice that was open to me.

There was the psychological fear, too, that many new mothers with careers still suffer from: if I step away, I'm going to lose momentum, I'm going to lose my job. I had to make sure my work was still up to scratch so I didn't attract criticism.

That meant, in those early days, I really, really felt the pressure because I was trying to be perfect at everything. A lot of women assume that the shock of having a baby will be the pain of the birth, but for me that wasn't it at all. Giving birth was no problem. For me, someone used to having so much energy, the shock was the utter exhaustion that I felt afterwards. I was up all night feeding Sophia, at work all day, and sleeping for about an hour and a half in every 24 hours. Until you have children, you live your life at the pace you want to live it, you work as hard as you want, you go to bed when you want. And suddenly there's this little baby saying, 'No, you're not going to sleep. Not for a while.'

In retrospect, there had been warning signs, in that I was exhausted towards the end of my pregnancy. Sometimes I'd be at my desk and just think, Oh, my God, I'm so tired I could fall asleep right here – but I wanted to make sure everything stayed business as usual. I remember my mother saying to me a few days after I'd had Sophia, 'You do know you've got a baby, don't you? You have to change.' But for six months I ignored that advice and just tried to carry on as normal, as though nothing had happened. I don't remember feeling guilty about Sophia; I do remember thinking that if effort was the measure then no one could try harder than I was trying. I had a room set up next to my office so that she and the nanny could come to work a couple of days a week, I breastfed her for the first few weeks. And I spent every night with her, most of it awake.

Sophia was one of those two-hour babies – I was up at night feeding her at ten o'clock, twelve o'clock, two o'clock, four o'clock and six o'clock. Then I would get up and go to work, come back and do it all over again. I didn't have a maternity nurse to do the night feeds because I was determined that if I wasn't going to be there during the day I was going to be there at night. I was determined to do it all.

So for six months I got more and more tired, until I felt like my head was in a cloud, as though there was a fog around me. If I did manage to get a night's sleep, things were even worse: it was almost impossible to get back into the usual sleepless pattern.

I didn't resent work but, looking back, I did want someone to let me off the hook. Just to say, 'You're so tired, look at you, go home, it's OK.' But no one did. My bosses were all men with wives at home to take care of the family, or men without children, and I think they had absolutely no idea what I was going through. When David Sullivan had his kids a few years later, he said to me, 'I don't know how you did it.'

There were some funny moments. I remember, soon after Sophia was born, sitting through a very tough four-hour meeting with five men, and afterwards I went to the loo and saw there were two huge round wet circles on my jacket over my breasts. Milk must have been leaking throughout the meeting, with the patches getting bigger and bigger, and none of them had said anything.

I'm not a moaner. I just grit my teeth and carry on. But after six months something snapped. I was on the verge of burn-out, totally exhausted. I couldn't carry on that way, so I said to Paul, 'You're going to have to do some of the night feeds, because if I don't get some sleep ...'

He said, 'Of course I will.' After two nights he was wailing, 'Oh it's so hard!'

Yes, I thought. Now you know.

From then on, Paul helped out more and things were easier. Paul's mother came over from Canada and spent three months with me, helping me get into a routine, and then Paolo arrived in 1998. This time I took six weeks off, a longer stretch, but nothing changed when I went back. Now and then I would have ideas about working a bit less, but there was always a crisis. In that respect, I envy people who run huge corporations with a massive amount of support staff, who just carry on regardless. It's completely different when you're running a smaller business, as I was, where you're the financial director, the marketing director, the sales director. You can't just walk away.

Still, if I were having my children now, I'd take as much maternity leave as I could, but I'd still work – which is possible now, because in the last 15 years communications have changed beyond recognition. Emails, mobile phones, BlackBerrys have transformed the way we can operate. Now, if you don't have to see someone face to face, you could be anywhere in the world – or in your living room with your baby. Those possibilities didn't really exist when I had my children.

Plus, it would be very different now anyway, because I wouldn't have that fear of losing my job, which I did in my twenties. Today, if I wanted to do things one way and the company I was working for said that wasn't good enough, I'd say, fine – and promptly leave. But in my twenties I didn't understand that that was an option. I was still proving myself. And most women don't have that choice anyway. You either need the money or, even if financially you can walk away, you're still tied psychologically. You love the job, or at least you need it in some way. But I've now got to the position, both financially and mentally, where I'm not scared of saying, 'No, I'm not doing that. That's not how I want to do it.'

So if my daughter, Sophia, decides to have children, I would definitely say to her, 'Remember, a career lasts a lifetime and you've got to have a period of calm to get over the storm. So what if you take six months off? The career will still be there when you're ready to go back to it.' I would certainly advise her to take time off to be with her new baby, and would want her to feel much more able to do that than I did. I hope that in years to come the guilt that women suffer will have gone and that taking time off will be seen as natural, expected and compulsory. I sincerely hope that attitudes have changed and people appreciate that it isn't unreasonable to give women time off to enjoy being a mother, without them feeling the fear, the guilt or the pressure to return to work quickly. Life goes on without you at home – but so does life in the office.

My advice to any ambitious woman who wants to have a baby is: just do it. And somehow it will work out. Take the maximum maternity leave, but keep your hand in. Keep in touch so people don't forget about you. Enjoy the time that you have off, but try to find a balance.

When you do go back, you'll find you have to fit your work into a shorter day. You have to be able to leave at a reasonable time, which means you slot the same amount of work into fewer hours. That was never a problem for me, to be honest. I made sure I was always prepared, so if I had to leave I could. I think that if you manage your business or department properly it shouldn't be a problem.

Everybody in my organisation knows what they are doing, which means that if one person falls off the production line, things wouldn't grind to a halt. It's about getting your business to run like a machine – information goes in, filters through the channels and the end product comes out perfectly. And once you've made it work like that, you don't have to stand over the machine every day. If you have to go home, it'll keep going.

So, I didn't find it hard to be more efficient, but I did find it difficult that my male counterparts were able to devote all their time to their careers because their wives took care of every-thing at home. In football, a lot of the business goes on out of hours. There are all sorts of networking evenings and I couldn't always get to those. No one picked me up on it, but I was aware of it.

Still, although people think it must have been harder for me because I had this big job, in a way it was easier because I had money and privileges. And the big difference between me and someone who's got a nine-to-five job, working for someone else, is that I'm the boss. When I was at Birmingham City and the children were young, if the nanny called and said, 'I think Paolo's got a bit of a cold,' I'd be in my car and at home twenty minutes later. I knew that if I wanted to go home I could – and I did when I needed to. No one at the office would say anything, as they knew I was not a slacker.

And I know that my children would say that I was always there. Once they started school, I always did the morning school run. I couldn't pick them up in the afternoon, but I was there for all the key things, and nothing would have got in the way of that. Prize-giving, the nativity play, sports day – the things that your children work towards all year. If they put on a show, it's for you. They take these things very seriously and I think it's so important to make time for them.

I did miss out on school holidays, but sometimes I'd ring up the nanny and say, 'Bring the kids in, I want to see them, bring them for lunch.' They would come in and we'd have lunch and they'd play in the office. As Sophia got older and had more homework, she would come into work with me and sit in my office to read and revise. We were in the same room, and that was good enough for me. Just having her physically near me.

It wasn't all about making them fit in with my routine, though. I loved having young children, being out with them and doing normal things. In the early days no one knew who I was really, so I could take Sophia or Paolo to the church group, the playground, the ball pen, have coffee with the other mums, and so on, without attracting any scrutiny. I can't imagine what it's like for someone like Victoria Beckham, who can't just go into a normal environment like that and be anonymous. Imagine not being able to take your kids for an ice-cream without people staring at you.

There's a lot said about the supposed divide between working and stay-at-home mums, but I've never experienced other mothers judging me negatively because I work. I think that whole mummy battle is a complete myth. In fact, I genuinely don't think other mums care if you work or not. I don't think they condemn those who are in that position. If they give any thought to it, maybe some stay-at-home mums sometimes wish they could drop their kids, go off and get a well-paid job too.

But, then, I've never got involved in the playground thing, or any of the politics that might be around it. There is always a group of mums who organise things, who get everybody together and run the PTA, and while for some this can be rewarding I've never been part of that. It's just not my thing, too many petty politics!

One playground incident, when my son was in primary school, sticks in my mind. Paolo has always been very popular, maybe because he's one of the oldest in the class and he's a like-able boy. One afternoon, I arrived to pick him up and my nanny was there too, because I wasn't sure if I'd make it in time. 'Something's happened,' she said. She told me that one of the other mothers wanted to have a word with me about Paolo, who was only about six at the time.

I went up and asked the mother what the issue was, to which she replied that her son was unpopular at school because Paolo didn't like him. 'You don't like my son, do you?' she asked Paolo directly, who was standing next to me.

'No, actually, I don't.' He just came straight out with it, the way an adult never would.

The other woman was about to say something else, but I said, 'Hang on a minute. I can't force my son to like your child or anybody else's, and I don't think Paulo is asking anything from you or your son.' I was furious. My children have been encouraged to be honest and say what they think – to have that sense of independence. She shut up.

That incident made me thankful I wasn't stuck at home fret-ting about the children's playtime or social lives. Does it really matter if you're not popular at six? Is that really what keeps you awake at night? Do you have to produce perfect, popular kids who get invited to all the parties? And what sort of pressure does that then heap on the children?

Of course, being a working mother brings its own headaches. One of the hardest things is that you have to be two people. You have to leave your work persona at the door when you get home: you can't take your problems home with you. I've seen lots of people having a difficult time at work, and it really can affect your whole life, leaving you with a sense of melancholy, even desperation or depression.

But, as a leader of the household, you're the heart of the home, and if you take those feelings in with you they will infect everyone in the house. You can't do it. So I have my home personality and my work personality. At work I am focused and driven, I have a set of standards that I want everyone to meet. I want to win things. I want to be in control of the company and ensure that everyone is striving for success. We don't look for the shortcuts; we do all things with integrity.

Whereas at home I'm always looking for the shortcuts. Can I stick the school shirts on the dryer instead of ironing them, can I force more stuff in the dishwasher? I'm laid back at home, a place where everyone – family, friends and guests – can relax and feel welcome. There are no rules, such as no shoes, or feet off the sofa, but at work rules are important, as are boundaries. Work Karren would not survive at home, and vice versa. And the vital trick? Not to allow one of these personalities to drain the life out of the other.

That means it's really important not to get stressed, to avoid reaching the point that you can't leave your work headaches in the office. Thankfully, I very rarely do. But I am still aware every day that having a career and having children is bloody hard. Anybody who says it's easy either has an awful lot of support or a very different attitude to guilt than most other mothers.

Women are not always honest about this, and I do think things would be easier for us all if successful women were to tell it as it is. If a successful woman goes on TV and gives the impression that you can be the perfect mother, the perfect businesswoman, the perfect wife, and so on, all at the same time, other women will think, Well, I'm never going to achieve that, so I won't do it at all. Or they will feel disheartened about what they are achieving.

The idea that any woman can have loads of children, run a billion-pound business, bake cakes and look fabulous is misleading. What people forget about a woman in that position is that she's got a chauffeur, a nanny, a housekeeper – an entire staff – behind her. When you get to that point, you can buy the sort of support network that means you can operate entirely on your terms. It's not like asking your mum, 'Can you pop in?' and if she can't do it you're screwed. If you've got that kind of support network, they're paid, they work and that's it.

I have had support, and I am happy to say so. We relied on a nanny until the children were ten and eight, after which Paul and I have managed it between ourselves. My mum and dad and my in-laws have been very helpful as well, as have my friends. No woman can operate without her friends.

But when we did have help it worked well. I was never jealous of my nanny; Sophia and Paolo were always my children. I'd ring them from work three times a day; I was there in the morning and home again early in the evening. It was never like you see in films, where the baby falls in love with the nanny. Who comes up with these plots? Are such things written to torture working mothers?

But I felt envious of my nanny in another way. As I was getting ready for work, she would be getting my daughter ready to go to the park. I wanted to be the one doing that – but I wanted my career as well. I wanted to be at home and I wanted to be at work too. Many working mothers will understand those mixed emotions.

Fundamentally, I didn't want to have to make a choice between those two aspects of my life – and didn't see why I should have to. I felt real envy of my male colleagues who could be at work all day knowing their wives were at home with the kids. So I concentrated on finding a way of making both areas of my life work, because it was so important to me, which meant paying for help.

In terms of childcare, my best piece of advice is that if you are fortunate enough to find someone who is right for you and your children, treasure them and respect them as a professional.

You need to recognise that this person allows you to go out to work every day. Without them none of it would hang together.

In the ten years that we used childcare, we had three nannies, which is a miracle. I know people who have gone through 30 or 40 in the same length of time, probably because they treated them like servants. I've seen women treat their nannies in the most appalling way – 'Do this, do that.' I didn't treat mine like that. It doesn't pay.

I made sure my nannies were properly looked after and, as a result, not once in all those years did any of them take a day off sick, even though one was heavily pregnant herself when she left. They knew that if they did it would completely throw me, and they were loyal. They were all three of them brilliant: they were dedicated, hardworking, and they respected my home life and didn't gossip (although, frankly, there was nothing to gossip about). They made my life possible, and they would have done anything for me because I would have done anything for them.

When it comes to choosing childcare, gut instinct is the best guide. If you're comfortable and the children are fine, that's as good as it gets. It's the same as balancing work and home: your kids will tell you when something's not working. If your childcare isn't right, your children won't be happy.

Of course I know that not everyone can afford the childcare they want. I was in a fortunate position, but one of the hardest barriers for women in work to surmount is getting access to affordable, high-quality childcare. The problem is obvious: if you're a working mum, you've got to leave your kids with somebody and you have to find the right sort of person or environment – local, easy, flexible, trustworthy and affordable. It's a tall order.

The government talks about wanting to get women into work, but many barely break even after they've paid for childcare. That's why I believe that there should be a tax allowance for childcare. After all, you can't go to work unless you pay for that service. It's like asking a taxi driver not to claim the cost of his taxi against his earnings – outrageous.

And every woman wants her child to have the best care possible. These days, most of us are having children older, and we're having fewer, and we want to give them the best we can. If you've got to dump them in a grubby nursery where the carers are changing all the time, it must be a nightmare.

But even a nanny won't be there all the time – nor would you want them to be, if you're anything like me. The reality is that if you want a family and a career, something has to give. For me, as I've said, that thing is my social life – I don't go out. Work and family are the two most important things in my life, and the only two things I have time for. Even when my children were young, and I had a nanny, I went to bed at eight o'clock every night. I didn't cook fancy food, I didn't have a social life, I just worked, saw the family and slept. That was the reality.

It might not sound like the reality you want. But any doubts I might have had that this was not the right path for me are long gone. The autumn of 2009, when I took over from Margaret Mountford as an adviser to Lord Sugar on *The Apprentice*, was incredibly busy. Filming the show was full on, and I was also selling Birmingham City to a Hong Kong consortium. I was up all night on the phone to Hong Kong and working on the deal, and all day I was filming. I didn't see the family all week. At times I felt as though I'd left home.

Then, quite abruptly, the business was sold, filming finished soon after, and for three months I didn't work at all. I found that equally difficult, being at home full-time. I was searching for things to do. Every cupboard in the house was perfectly cleared out. Then, when someone came home, I'd find myself saying, 'Look what I did to the airing cupboard!', and they'd say, 'So?' And I'd think, Yes, actually, so what?

Normally, I'd get home from work, stick a few steaks on the barbecue and put a bit of rice on to boil, but I found myself slaving away over recipe books to make a beautiful meal. Then the family would come in and say, 'Ooh, I don't like the look of that,' and I'd feel devastated.

It got so I couldn't remember how I'd managed to run a home and a business. Some days I wouldn't get out of my dressing gown till two o'clock in the afternoon. Someone would come round, the phone would ring, I'd have to pick the kids up – it made me realise that I needed to be busy, and that the busier I am the more organised I am.

In the end I felt as though I had lost my identity. I would make business calls, and the person on the other end would say, 'Where are you calling from?'

'My living room,' I'd reply. I didn't have a business title or even a work address to identify myself, since my recent projects were finished. I remember having a conversation with Margaret Mountford about it, saying to her that I didn't know how to describe myself on an application form, and she said, 'Just put down company director' – which, of course, I still was. At the time, I was a board director at Mothercare. But I hadn't thought about that as my identity.

I guess that society teaches us to define ourselves by what we do. Looking back at that time, I wonder if that is how men feel, when they're looking after their children while their partner works. That isn't right, of course, but when you meet people it's often what you do that defines you, and for men I think it's even harder. When they say, 'I don't work,' I wonder if they imagine people are judging them, thinking they're living off someone or just lazy.

That's not how I see it. Being at home can sometimes be a thankless task. No one says, 'Well done – today you unloaded the dishwasher, good for you. And you did the ironing.' If you're at home, it's expected that you'll do these things, but you don't get any sort of acknowledgement for it, and the whole thing is bloody hard work. In many ways I couldn't wait to get back to the office. For me, personally, it sometimes felt like being a great chef and only ever making beans on toast. I didn't feel I had the opportunity to demonstrate what I was good at, and that was horrible.

So, I finally had my time at home with the family and I learnt that I definitely needed to work as well. It's different if you have a job that's not very rewarding and you do it just for the money. If you're there because you have to be there, while you really want to be with your children, that's terribly hard – but it's different for me, it's not as black and white as that.

I love what I do. I get a real buzz from going in, solving problems, working out strategy, motivating my people. I get into the office and I don't want to leave, and then I go home and I don't want to leave. I love them both.

The problem is, I have to admit, that I've never managed to get the split between the two quite right. It's always a balancing act, even now.

My usual answer when people ask me how I've made sure I've got the balance right is that I let the children be the judge. If you're not spending enough time at home, your children will tell you. Every mother knows when their children need more of them, because when you've not been around enough they become more demanding and start playing up to get your attention. But, of course, that isn't the end of the story: even when you know you need to be with them more, it isn't always possible.

For example, I started my job at West Ham in east London at the beginning of 2010, and my time is now divided between

London and Birmingham. As I've said, the idea was to work at the club three days a week, which would have meant two nights in London, and spend the rest of the time in Birmingham with my family. That was a nice idea, but it hasn't worked out quite like that.

Something always comes up – the Olympic Stadium plans are in jeopardy, the club's been relegated. When you're looking for a new manager, you can't always say, 'Well, actually, I can only meet you Monday.' The result is that I spend most of my time now in London, and it's too much.

I find it so hard to be away from the family all week. In fact, I'm not sure how long I can go on doing it. I miss them and I know they miss me. They need me to be around more than I am at the moment, and they're telling me so. Not always directly, but one of my children will ring up and ask, 'Which day is it that you're coming home again?' and I realise I've been away too long.

And all the time I'm in London a part of me is saying, 'Why am I working myself to death when I don't get to see my children?' I'll ring my husband in the morning and he'll say, 'I'm just getting the kids into the car to go to school.' I'll say, 'OK, call me when you get home,' and 10 minutes go past, 15, and he's forgotten. I'm just too far away. They know I'm not there. Life's going on without me.

In my own way, I've always been able to make things work before. No matter how difficult, there's always been a path through, but physical distance makes it impossible right now. I don't know what the answer is yet – I'm here, they're up there, I need to be here, they want me to be there, I want to be there. What's going to happen? I'll have to find a way.

I'm home at weekends, that's true, but as the children get older things change. We don't have family time in quite the same way any more. On a Saturday, the kids want to go out with their friends, they want their friends over, they want to go to the cinema. So I'll say, 'What are we doing today?', and they'll say, 'I don't know what you're doing but I know what I'm doing.' It's just what happens as kids get older. If I asked, 'Do you want to go to the zoo?' they'd look at me as if I was a lunatic.

I am tempted, though. As I write, my daughter's nearly 16 and I'm terrified that she'll get to 18, move out, and I'll still be waiting for everything to slow down. And then I'll be like one of those mad, horrible mothers who doesn't want their children to leave home – I can see it!

So, it's not always easy to get the balance right, but at the same time, I think you can wait for ever to achieve it when you need to just get on with your life and do your best.

Everybody's balance is different, but if you're worried more about getting the balance right than actually living your life, you've got the balance wrong. You'll have to find your own way through, between work and family, and if you want both, you have to make sacrifices. It's called compromise: both aspects of your life have to give a little so you can find a middle ground. I could have stayed at home and been with my children 24/7 – but I would probably have been utterly miserable, and I honestly don't think my kids would have been any different.

At the end of the day, from two years nine months onwards, children are in nursery, then school, and I've tried to make the most of that time to carve out my career. Sometimes it's spilt over a bit and, equally, sometimes my family life has spilt into my working life. I just try to do my best. I'm very close to my children, we have a good relationship and they know there's nothing I wouldn't do for them.

Sometimes you won't get it right. Then, you've just got to accept that you're doing your best and your best will be good enough. If your kids know that you love them, that you try to make a good living for them, that you're there when you can be, that you're there for the important things but also that you want to be a role model to them, so they know that hard work and a career are important – then you're on the right track.

Looking back, the one thing I do find is that because of everything I've been juggling all their lives, sometimes it feels that everything merges into one. I do feel sad about that and, yes, there are moments when I think I'm a terrible mother.

All mothers feel some guilt at some time, but most of us know it's pointless. In fact, rationalising it, I can't understand what the guilt is about. I know that, as a mother, if I haven't been able to do what needs doing, I've always made sure that someone's there who can do it. But there is a drip-drip of guilt coming at you from the outside (mainly the media), on top of what women do to themselves. You need to develop some resilience to it, because it will hurt you. It's insidious.

And as long as you feel in your own heart that you've done your best, then I don't see why anyone else should judge what's right for you and your family. I've known footballers from broken homes, whose father is in prison, whose mother has died from drugs, they're in a gang, there's been a shooting – now that's a tough childhood. Trying to have a career is not a crime, and I want my daughter and my son to feel equally able to go out and forge their path in life.

I always say to Sophia, who is doing her GCSEs, that it's important to work hard, but it's difficult for her – there are so many distractions at her age. A year or so ago I remember telling her: 'This isn't your life. You're 14. You won't even remember being 14 when you're 18, let alone when you're my age. You think this is your life, but it's not. This is the route to getting a life. You get a life when you get the results you want and a career you can be happy doing, when you're earning your own money, you've got independence and you're making your own decisions.

'But how good a career you get is really based on what you get now, and how much effort you're prepared to put into it. And these boys you're hanging around with and interested in, you won't even remember their names in two years' time, let alone five, but by then it'll be too late to go back and put in the effort.'

She's listened – so far! – and as I write, she's just had another round of results, in which she got three As, two A*s and a B in her exams. I told her, 'You've got a great life ahead of you – and whatever happens I'm here to help you.'

That doesn't mean following the same route as me, necessarily. Even though I didn't go to university, I would love it if my kids did. I'm sure lots of parents feel the same. My theory is that, since many women are becoming mothers later, when they've got a bit more money, a bit more time, as a result, perhaps they have higher expectations for their children than if they'd had them when they were relatively carefree and penniless.

And while I know it's not the only route to success – it wasn't mine – I would really like one of my children to be a professional of some sort, to have a real skill. It has niggled at me all my life that I can't write down one qualification on my CV. Yes, I have four A levels, but that's not really what I'm talking about. I mean something more tangible, like being a lawyer. I do now have a doctorate – honorary – but I would have liked to know when I started out that, actually, if it didn't all work out for me in the path I was forging, I could go and earn a living as a beautician or a hairdresser or whatever. But I had no skills. I couldn't even type. All I had was my personality and my drive.

I was confident in my abilities, but when I was younger I worried about what would happen if I didn't make a go of something. That helped me to stick with whatever I ended up doing, so it wasn't wholly bad. But I'd like it to be different for my children.

I suppose you always want things to be a bit smoother for those who come after you – and, for me, that includes mothers who work.

CH.9
MY BRUSH
WITH DEATH

Work, marriage, children – that seems quite enough to be dealing with. But life will still throw you a curveball, out of nowhere.

In 20 years of working I don't think I ever took a full day off sick. I'm just not an ill person. And on the rare occasions when I don't feel well, I just get on with it. I'm strong and resilient, physically as well as mentally, and I suppose that made me feel invincible.

But that changed after I woke up one morning in 2006, with blotches all over my skin and my body visibly swelling. Paul just looked at me and said: 'Oh, my God.' He immediately drove me to A&E, where the staff were visibly shocked. They rushed me through to the wards and put me on a drip, and after about 12 hours they had it under control. It was an allergic reaction, they told me, but they didn't know what had caused it.

My first thought was, I have to deal with this – I travel a lot and don't have time to be worrying about whether something I'm eating has peanuts in it, or whatever it was that had set me off. The thought of packing my own sandwiches for every journey I made filled me with dread. I had to find out what I was allergic to and resolve it.

At the time I was on the board of Sport England, the government agency, and one of the directors had a daughter who ran a preventive-medicine clinic. He recommended I go there. I duly went and had a day of tests for everything you can imagine, plus an MRI scan. My whole body was examined, from the tip of my toes to the top of my head. But I had a Channel 4 board meeting that afternoon, so I didn't wait for the results. As soon as the tests were finished, off I went and didn't think anything more about it.

Reality hit the following day. I was in my office in Birmingham, when the doctor phoned and said he needed to speak to me. It sounded important so I took the call. 'I'm sorry to have you tell you,' he said, 'but you've got a brain aneurysm.'

I had no idea what a brain aneurysm was, so I just said, 'Oh.'

'You'll need to see a specialist,' he said,

'Okay,' I said.

'Can you go tomorrow?'

I started to get worried. 'Is it serious?'

'Yes, I'm afraid it is.' And then he explained a bit about what an aneurysm is: a bulge in an artery of the brain where blood gathers. The chances were that I was born with it. I asked him whether it was something I could live with, but he said, no, I needed to have an operation – soon.

'Is it so serious I might die if I put off seeing a specialist until next week?' I asked.

'You could die crossing the road,' was his answer.

As soon as I rang off, I got on to the Internet. The more I read, the more scared I became. Most people who have a brain aneurysm have no idea, I learnt – there are no symptoms and the aneurysm can sit there for years, for a whole lifetime, even. But it's like a time bomb in your head, in that at any moment it might burst, which could kill you or leave you disabled. Many people only find out they have a brain aneurysm when it bursts, so I am incredibly lucky that I happened to have that scan.

Receiving that sort of news is like being sucked into a tunnel. I tried to do what I always do – to focus on what needed to be done, rather than feel self-pitying – but it wasn't easy. I had to tell Paul and my parents, but for some reason I felt really embarrassed about telling anybody. Probably because I didn't want a fuss – I was not used to being ill, or the subject of sympathy. I even thought about whether to wait until after I'd seen the specialist, when I knew more about what was involved, but in the end I told Paul. His reaction was the same as mine: 'What's an aneurysm?'

The next day we went to London to see a neurologist, one of the best. The clinic booked me in. It was all still sinking in – I remember saying to this specialist, 'Look, this is obviously a routine thing for you. Please just get on and do what needs doing.' But he told me that it was not routine, that the brain is a complicated computer of wires – one snip of the wrong wire and it's all over.

All I wanted was reassurance, for him to say, 'Yes, it's serious, but now we've found it we can sort it out. This is what I do every day, so don't worry at all.' But he actually said, 'I'm afraid you'll have to come to terms with the fact that you'll never have children.' When I told him I already had two, he said it was a miracle I'd survived the raised blood pressure of pregnancy. That was when I thought, Oh no, this really is serious.

I also knew very quickly that this man was not the one I wanted to do the operation. I didn't like him. I felt as though I was just a number for him, an interesting procedure, and I thought, If I'm going to put my life in somebody else's hands then it's going to be somebody who doesn't just see me as patient number one, two, three or four.

At the same time making the decision wasn't as simple as that: while I was thinking, I don't like this man, I was also thinking, Do you have to like him? The important thing is that he's the best – does it matter if you don't want to be friends for ever? But then I thought, If I don't like him, he probably doesn't like me and he won't care about the outcome enough – he doesn't understand that I've got a family. My mind was whirring. I was struggling to stay focused and make decisions, because my head said this man was the best, but my gut instinct was that he wasn't for me. It was so hard. The stakes were so high and it was such a shock to me that my normally very clearcut style of decision-making didn't work. To follow my gut instinct or my head, that was the dilemma.

But then, as I left his office, I said to him: 'Out of interest, if your wife had this condition and you weren't allowed to operate, who would she get?' And he said, 'Only I can do it.' Then I knew I should go with my gut: it wasn't going to be him. A professional who could not recommend anyone but himself was too arrogant in my book. He'd rather let his wife die than find someone else? I bet his wife wouldn't agree with that!

So I rang around a few people, looking for a recommendation, and one surgeon's name kept coming up: Ian Sabin at the Wellington Hospital, a large private hospital in north London. And yes, I do think it would have been slower on the NHS. I was with Bupa and they were fantastic, and not because I was who I was. They showed real compassion for my situation, made sure I had the surgeon and the hospital I wanted, and continued my aftercare at that hospital even though later they had changed their policy about locations and doctors. Healthcare insurance is the best insurance you can get, so get the very best you can afford. Not having to worry about when I'd have my treatment, or where, was a blessing.

Anyway, we saw Ian next. I knew immediately that this time I'd found the right person. I liked him instantly and I still do. The first thing he said was, 'I know this is very difficult – I can't imagine how it feels,' and he had put my mind at rest. It felt right that he would look after me – and I understand why people can fall a little bit in love with their surgeons. A calm approach coupled with ability is very important in a doctor. Ian had both in abundance.

Choosing a surgeon was only the first tough decision I had to make, however. The world of serious illness is all about choices and risks, and that is very difficult. If your arm's broken, they strap it up and off you go, but with something more complicated like a brain aneurysm it's very different. There were two treatments on offer, and each one came with a cata-strophic reason not to choose it.

The first option was a craniotomy: the surgeon would cut open my skull and operate directly on my brain, attaching a clip to the aneurysm to stop blood flowing into it. The second was 'coiling': a wire is inserted, via the groin, up through the heart and neck into the artery, where it coils up inside the aneu-rysm, choking it off. A craniotomy, which is the more invasive procedure, can lead to a stroke. With coiling, the aneurysm may burst while the wire is being inserted. So there I was, being asked to make a balanced judgement between two things I'd only found out about the day before, either of which could lead to my death. I'm used to taking risks and making decisions under pressure but this was completely out of the realms of my experience.

There was a third option, of course. I could have chosen not to have anything done – after all, I'd lived with the aneurysm for many years, maybe all my life, and it was possible I could have lived out my natural lifespan without it killing me. Not all aneurysms burst, and of those that do, there is a one in three chance that you'll be completely unaffected. But there is also a one in three chance that it will kill or leave you disabled. I couldn't live like that, knowing that at any moment the aneurysm could blow my life apart. But should I choose the craniotomy or the coiling?

Paul and my dad were with me when I saw Ian Sabin, but they had different views. Paul thought I should definitely go for the major surgery – the craniotomy – 'because once it's done it's done for ever'. The problem with the alternative, coiling, is that it often has to be repeated, as it's not always 100 per cent successful on the first occasion. My dad was saying, 'But if the craniotomy is so successful, why did they invent another way of dealing with it?' Meanwhile I sat between them, not knowing who was right.

Of course, in the end, I decided I had to make up my own mind. I have my own way of dealing with things, and I trust myself. I'm much better at making my own decisions than I am at being talked into something. Ian Sabin's specialism was the major surgery, but he told me about the coiling alternative and recommended a specialist, Paul Butler. I had both doctors explain their technique, and why they thought it would be best for me.

Still, I felt I didn't have the knowledge to make this life-or-death decision. How was I supposed to choose? So I relied on the sort of techniques I'd use to guide me in business. I'm a great believer in letting experts make the decisions, so I went back to them both and said I wanted them to get together and decide between them which procedure had the best chance of success.

They decided on the coil. Paul Butler said he would do the operation but Ian Sabin would be there in case of complications, should the aneurysm rupture during the operation. And I said, 'Fine.'

That was that. The surgery was booked for the following week. If it had been possible, I would have had it that very afternoon, but it wasn't an option. I just didn't want time to think.

In the meantime, Paul and I went back to Birmingham. It wasn't the best few days of my life. I prayed a lot. When you're faced with death, it's comforting to allow yourself to think that there might be something afterwards. I think that gives people hope and takes away the fear. Yet at the same time I remember thinking that for me the afterlife was my children – they're what you leave behind on earth.

I tried not to let myself think it wouldn't work. I was worried, but it wasn't for me that I was most scared. The real torture was the thought of Sophie and Paolo. They were still so young – Sophia was ten at the time, and Paolo eight – and the thought of leaving them was horrendous. I was haunted by the thought that someone else would be living in my house, bringing up my children, be it a family member or a new mother for them. That was what kept me awake. Not that I'd die, but what would happen if I wasn't there.

I never told them what was happening. They knew I was going to London to have an operation but they didn't know what was wrong or how serious it was. I just said it was something routine. When the news got out, my nanny had to keep turning the radio down so they wouldn't hear about it. But I think that, underneath, they knew. They were unsettled. Children sense when something is very wrong.

I had to spend five days in hospital being monitored before the surgery, feeling like a fraud. I was feeling perfectly well, and with an aneurysm there is no outward sign that anything is wrong. The floor I was on at the Wellington was for brain and spinal injuries, so the people around me were seriously ill, while I was there in a tracksuit, sitting around, watching telly, popping in and out for some fresh air, with lots of friends and family coming and going.

But while, physically, I felt fine, mentally, it was good for me to spend that time there, because it helped me come to terms with what was happening. I was there, that was my situation, and I had to deal with it. I would probably have not been much good at doing anything else. It wouldn't have been easy to worry about the new grass that was going on the pitch when I knew I was about to have a major operation.

I had to let people – colleagues, family, friends – know what was happening, but I would have preferred to keep it to myself. I felt awkward about it; I am private person at heart. And I quickly learnt that people don't know how to deal with illness. The worst thing is their faces when they ask, 'Are you OK?' And they'd hang around my bed, just sitting there.

The problem was that, as I'm a strong woman, everyone thought I'd be all right about it, that I'd take everything on the chin, that I'm endlessly resilient. And probably I came over like that. But, actually, I did want an arm put around me without any fuss. There's definitely a way to behave when someone's ill: you're there to keep their spirits up. I might have looked strong, but I found my fear quite difficult to cope with. Even Paul wasn't as supportive as he might have been, and he knows I think that. He was at Derby County at the time: they'd sacked their manager and he was acting as caretaker. On one occasion when he came in to visit me, he said, 'Could you help me make a few calls to get some loan players in?' And I did, like the silly cow I am. I remember thinking, Hello, I'm in bed, I've got an aneurysm, I'm going to have a massive operation!

Ultimately, I'd rather have been on my own, getting through it. And if I ever get ill again I don't think I'll tell anybody at all, I'll just deal with it myself.

The person who dealt with it best, for me, was my solicitor, Henri Brandman, who is also one of my closest and dearest friends. In the morning he would nip into the hospital, bring me a newspaper and say, 'How are you doing? Everything all right?', stay five minutes and go. Then, in the evenings when he'd finished work, he'd pop in and he'd have picked up a book or cut out an interesting article from a different paper; we'd have a laugh about it and then he'd go. He was just what I needed.

And then the day came. I walked to the operating theatre – I was adamant that I didn't want to be wheeled. Looking back, a lot of that time is very hazy, but one moment is crystal clear. The operating theatre was a big room filled with machines, scanning equipment, to monitor my brain. And I remember this so well: there was an observation window into the room, and as I walked in for this very serious operation, not knowing what the outcome would be, there was a guy sitting behind the window eating a sandwich. I remember thinking, Oh, well, life goes on.

They tied me to the bed, a horrible sensation, and then ... blackness.

As soon as I came round I asked, 'Did you get it?' I was worried I'd have to go through it all again, but they said everything was fine. The doctor told me that the next 24 hours were the most important – that if I survived, my chances would be dramatically better. So I lay there and quite literally watched the clock for 24 hours. It was a long day.

Thankfully, my intensive-care nurse was a lovely woman, who sat with me for hours. She was a Liverpool supporter and talked about Liverpool for hour after hour. Under normal circumstances, I'd have been saying, 'Oh my God, give it a rest,' but I was desperate for her to keep talking because I wanted the time to pass. She was absolutely lovely – and she never shut up. I was so grateful to her. There were two beds in intensive care and I never saw the guy in the bed next to mine because there was a curtain between us. But I do remember at one point he was saying, 'Water, water,' and the nurse said to me, 'Listen to him, he never shuts up!' It was so funny that I laughed out loud. God, it was good to be alive.

Paul, meanwhile, was asleep in the chair. There I was, watching the clock, hoping to survive 24 hours, and he was asleep. At one point I said to him sarcastically, 'Why don't you go up to my hospital room so you can sleep properly?'

'What a good idea,' he said, and off he went. I was not pleased!

But the 24 hours slowly ticked past. And then another week passed and I was told I could go home – with a caution. The key was, they told me, to keep as still as possible while the coils were embedding themselves into my brain, so on the way back to Birmingham we drove really slowly to avoid every lump and bump in the road. Of course, people thought we were just pootling along like Sunday drivers and were tooting us to go faster. I wanted to shout out of the window, 'I've just had brain surgery, you twat!'

The doctors told me I needed to take three months off work, and it was no effort to stay away, but in the end I only took six weeks. I felt fine and also I was under pressure to return. I remember very little about those weeks recuperating at home, apart from feeling tired all the time. My mother-in-law came over from Canada to look after me for a week, and my own mother came up with my dad, so I had plenty of support.

There were some weird side-effects, though. I'd have a sensation that was like someone sticking a pin into the side of my head, and feel as though my brain was about to explode, then it was as if the pin was being withdrawn. And I experienced waves when I felt as if I wasn't in the room. Later, when they looked at my brain scan, it showed that I'd had millions of mini-strokes – literally, millions – and I can only imagine that that was what I'd felt. Six months later, when I had my next brain scan, almost all of them had repaired themselves. It was amazing.

I never did discover what allergy it was that had sent me off to get all those tests. I think there were probably a few other things wrong as well, but the aneurysm was overwhelmingly worse. Once I'd dealt with that, I couldn't bring myself to go back.

But I do still have regular check-ups to find out how my brain is. For the first three years, I had to go back every 12 months, but now it's a bit more casual. I was due to be checked again in 2011, but I decided to wait another year. I saw my surgeon, Ian, and he said that would be all right. Apparently, at this stage, the chances of anything going wrong are the same for me as for anyone else. And I find the process difficult. My scans are always in August, and I find, come July, I start think-ing about it. It weighs on my mind. I'm one of those people who, when I close the door, it's closed – that's how I cope with these things. I've closed that door on that chapter in my life now and I'm reluctant to reopen it.

Some people, I think, when they face a situation similar to mine, make all sorts of vows about how they're going to change their life if they come through it, but I didn't feel like that. After the operation, Ian was very clear. He said, 'You've had the operation, you've had the best possible result, now don't think about it and get on with your life.' And I don't, as it's very good advice. I don't want to spend the rest of my life looking over my shoulder.

And I'm really not, to a degree that might surprise you. I was in Solihull town centre recently when a woman came running up to me and said, 'My daughter's got a brain aneurysm.' Of course, I said, 'Oh, my God, I'm so sorry,' but I had no idea why she was telling me. And then I remembered: it was because I'd had one. That lady told me she was worried because her daughter couldn't get on with her life, she was so depressed, and I can see how that could happen, when you can't stop thinking about it. I think the key to getting over an illness is to look forward.

Of course the experience changed me. Remember, my operation was just a matter of days after I had first found out anything was wrong. Just two weeks earlier, my life had been on one course when this bomb landed and caused havoc. An event like that shows you that you really have no idea what's going on in your body. It was a huge wake-up call, and at the heart of it was the horrible truth that life doesn't last for ever. An experience like that makes you reassess what is important. It made business seem irrelevant.

But it's a funny thing. You come away knowing that most of the things we worry about don't matter, that there are far bigger things in life. Yet it's surprising how quickly you slip back into normality. I remember, soon after the operation, being interviewed by a young woman journalist, and she'd had an aneurysm too, but a different type: hers was a cluster aneurysm that couldn't be corrected. It was always going to be there and at any moment she could have a major haemorrhage. We talked about the effect that having such an illness has on you and I said to her, 'You think about the things you worried about in the past and none of that seems important.'

She said, 'Oh, it won't be long before you're back worrying about all the same old trivial things.' I thought, No, that won't happen, but of course it did. Somehow you go back into your routine.

Still, being ill changed me fundamentally, and I think it shows with the big things. The decisions I make about work are affected by that experience. Now, if something isn't working, or if the balance between work and my family is skewed, I think I could have died five years ago, so why don't I do what I want to do? You don't stop worrying about the trivial things, but you do live in the moment that bit more.

In fact, it sounds odd, but in an ideal world everyone would have a near-death experience that turns out all right. It teaches you an awful lot about yourself. It brought it home to me that, when the chips are down, you can only rely on yourself. It's true – no one knows you, and what you need, better than you. The things in life that have never let me down are my career and me.

And it teaches you the importance of doing the things you want to do. About aiming high and asking a lot from life. Is getting up at eight and going to a factory to a job that bores you a good deal? With a bit more effort, you could have a much better life. My brush with death made me think about what *I* want to do and how *I* want to do it.

After all, we don't always get another chance.

CH.10
TIME FOR MY CLOSE-UP
MY TV CAREER

Life will take you in some unexpected directions, I know that for sure. But sometimes they will be welcome, and among these I would include my television work.

When you're always the boss, it can be nice to be part of someone else's team – and that's one of the things I love about my role on *The Apprentice*. Over the years I have done quite a bit of TV work, but I haven't always enjoyed it. By now, I know my strengths and my weaknesses and I know what my specialism is: it's business. So I was thrilled to be asked to be on my favourite TV show, and I love doing it. *The Apprentice* is a fantastic and unique mix of business and entertainment. For me, working on the show is something different, fun, and a complete contrast to my day job. My philosophy is that variety in life keeps you interested and interesting.

I was a big fan of *The Apprentice* long before I got involved in the show. I loved watching the tasks and the exposure of people's business skills – or lack of them. I also enjoyed the edge of madness that erupts in the competition to become Lord Sugar's apprentice. The show is very popular with all sorts of people, not just those in the business world, and I think that's because it's truly genuine. Everything you see is real, but it's not a reality show. There are no scripts, no pre-planning, no one pulling strings to make sure these people go down this track and those people go down that one. What happens is what happens, and I'm sure viewers like and appreciate the raw honesty of the approach.

When we walk into the boardroom, Alan Sugar – Alan to me, Lord Sugar to you! – doesn't have notes and there's no autocue. It's all spontaneous. So I have no idea what he's going to say or who he's going to say it to. I have no idea who's going to be fired. Sometimes I'm hanging on to my desk because the tension in the boardroom is so intense. And because it's not rehearsed, the emotion is genuine. He handles the contestants with such skill, particularly the kids on *Young Apprentice*, the spin-off show for candidates aged 16 and 17 years old. It's difficult firing young people. They don't always have the inner confidence you gain as you get older, and he deals with it so delicately: when he fires them, they don't lose their dignity. The adult candidates are not always so lucky, of course!

Everybody on the show respects Alan. That's because he knows how hard they work, from the runner picking up the coffee to the series producer in charge of the whole shebang. Alan knows it's their life's work, and that the whole show hinges on him – if he doesn't get it right, nothing else will be right. He takes that responsibility very seriously and does everything he can to make sure the show is excellent. And, of course, there's an added incentive for him to take the whole process seriously. At the end of the series he either has to go into business with one of these people or he has to employ them, so he's not looking for the jokers, weirdoes and freaks who make good TV. He's looking for proper businesspeople.

As his advisers on the show, Nick Hewer and I are the only ones on set who call Alan by his first name, although when we first started filming I'd forget sometimes and call him Lord Sugar. Then he'd roll his eyes and laugh and say, 'Call me Alan.' The three of us get on very well. For the last two years, we have filmed the *Young Apprentice* show first and then, after a short break, the adult series. It's been a bit like boarding school: we're with each other all the time, then we have a sort of half-term break, then we're together again. In fact, the three of us go out a lot when we're filming because we finish quite late. We'll grab a meal – and then, of course, get papped and chased down the bloody road. But I can see why the press might like to get a photo of the show's panel in a different setting to the boardroom. Well, they can try!

It was obvious that Alan and I would click, I suppose. He is probably the straightest talker I've ever met – the person you're least likely ever to make small talk with. He believes what he believes, no matter how un-PC it is. He would never think, What should I say?, always, What do I want to say? We don't always agree but he has earned the right to his opinion. He is also incredibly self-motivated – he knows exactly what he wants and he does exactly what he wants, and there's something awe-inspiring about it.

What he has really taught me is, as I mentioned before that the toughest thing about being a success is that you have to keep on being a success. You look at him and think, With all the money you have, the yachts, the houses and the planes, why aren't you living on a beach somewhere? But his personal drive for *continued* excellence in everything he does is a key reason why he is so successful. His desire to succeed has not been diminished with his success. It's well-known that in life, there are maximisers and satisfiers. Alan is not satisfied with average; he is only interested in maximising his ability to keep achieving, to keep caring about what he does.

Funnily enough, I'd known him for years before I got involved in *The Apprentice*, through the world of football. He bought Tottenham Hotspur just before I went to Birmingham City, and I watched what he did there with a lot of admiration. Many people talk about making a difference, but not a lot of people do it, and he really did make a difference to his football club. Yet he has talked about those years at Spurs as quite a dark experience for him, and I can understand why. Football can be very hard to break into. As an industry, it can be difficult for businesspeople coming from another area – Alan's background was more computers and electronics – to get their heads around because not much of it makes sense.

Football is not often run like a business, let alone thought of as a business. The supporters have a lot to say about the way the team is run, the players' performances, how the board operates, while the press has an opinion on everything. The people power – the supporter factor – can be a shock. Sometimes you just can't get it right. If you buy Beckham, they say you're a cheapskate because you didn't buy Messi too. And the supporters don't like people who come in and tell it how it is – and, of course, Alan did that. Then there are some shady characters whom Alan would not have enjoyed dealing with: agents, chancers who have got into football who, if they were not selling players, would be selling double glazing or second-hand cars. Basically, not the sort of people with integrity that Alan would want to deal with.

Towards the end of his time at Spurs he was getting an awful lot of criticism from the supporters. Once, when Birmingham were playing Spurs, I was in the boardroom there and, through the window, I could see this mob baying for him. It was nasty. His wife's face told me she was thinking, Why are we here? What are we doing this for? This is madness.

I felt sorry for him because he'd done a great job, and would have continued to do a great job. The next day I wrote a piece for the *Sun* saying that the Spurs supporters were chasing out the best friend they'd ever had. I said that I didn't think they understood the fundamental points that (a) he loved the club and (b) he could support his love for the club financially. In those days, Spurs spent more money in the transfer market than most other clubs put together. I think he appreciated what I had written, because from that point on we were friends.

I remember the call I had from him about joining *The Apprentice*. It was my daughter's birthday and we were having her party at a farm, of all places, so I answered the phone knee-deep in muck beside some goats. Alan got straight to the point: 'Margaret Mountford is thinking of leaving the show – she wants to further her studies (in the study of ancient documents – Margaret has a very sharp mind.) If she did, would you be interested in taking over from her? You have to think about it really carefully, because it's a huge commitment.'

I didn't need to think about it. 'Yes, I'd love to.' But a couple of days later he phoned again and said, 'Margaret has decided to stay on, so we don't need you after all.' I thought, Well, I've never been fired before I've been hired before, but thank you anyway.

And while I didn't get to be one of Alan's two advisers at that point, I was one of the guest interviewers on the 2008 and 2009 series who grill the final five contestants and give their opinions to Alan. That was interesting. You know nothing about the candidates – all you get is their CVs – and you have to investigate, checking what they have and haven't done against what they say they've done. There are a lot of discrepancies on those CVs! Most of the contestants have put some outrageous things on their application forms to get into the show, and then it all comes back to haunt them. I found their current or past employer's report most interesting: one told us that a candidate was unreliable, always late and had the worse excuses – that his cat had been run over (he didn't own a cat) or that he had dropped his house keys down the drain. That made me laugh. Then there was the female contestant who said she had a very special skill: the gift of intuition. Well, she didn't seem to intuit that I wasn't very impressed!

After trawling through their paperwork, we have a face-to-face interview with each candidate. Now, when this section is televised, the viewers know each candidate really well. They know their strengths and weaknesses and what sort of person they are because they have been watching them for weeks, but the interviewers have no idea. When a candidate walks into that room, I have never set eyes on them before. Still, we're talking about the final five at this stage, so they've all got something going for them, and some stand out immediately as exceptionally good.

The first time I did the interviews, for the 2008 series, that person was Claire Young, a Yorkshire woman who was nicknamed the 'Rottweiler'. Claire really impressed me because she knew so much about her business. Most people who work for a big organisation – in her case, Superdrug – can't tell you anything about it outside the department they work in. They don't know how many brands there are, what the global reach is, what profits the company makes – they don't know anything. Claire knew everything. I told Alan in the boardroom, 'If you don't give her a job I will,' and then, of course, she didn't win the series. He phoned me up afterwards and said, 'I hope now you're going to honour your promise and offer her a job,' and I did. She didn't come because she wanted to pursue a career in the media.

All in all, it was an experience I really enjoyed. And, eventually, Alan phoned and said, 'Margaret is definitely leaving this time – definitely, definitely, definitely. Would you like the job?' Again, he warned me to think carefully because the show is such a full-on commitment. We met to have a long chat and he said that, basically, it would mean twelve weeks away from home, working constantly. I knew I wanted to do it, but before I agreed I discussed it with Paul and the children. I told them it was going to mean twelve weeks' filming and that, on my days off from that I'd be in the office at Birmingham City taking care of things there, so I would hardly be coming home at all during that period. 'Everyone has to agree, because if, halfway through, you say to me you don't like it, I can't then break that commitment,' I warned them. But they said, 'Oh, no, no, we really want you to do it, go for it, it'll be great fun.'

And it was – but Alan was right to warn me. Filming is hard work. On the first episode I ever filmed, Nick Hewer and I were looking at our call sheets – the schedules they give you – and I said, 'Look, Nick, the task starts at midnight. How interesting.' That was when we realised it meant us, too, not just the contestants. And we filmed that first task for 46 hours straight through. I remember thinking, God, when Alan said this was tough, he wasn't exaggerating.

The TV role is very demanding, a huge commitment in time, energy, stamina and concentration. Nick and I have to be watching and concentrating all the time. We don't make any decisions about who does what on the tasks, or who should be fired: our job is purely to observe. But that's a big job. Alan is not present during the tasks, so we are his eyes and ears. We have to be able to tell him exactly who made a decision that led to any particular outcome. The idea is that when the candidates start the buck-passing in the boardroom, Alan can jump in and say, 'No, you were the one who said that was the right thing to do, not so-and-so.' It involves taking huge amounts of notes. I find I very rarely look at what's happening. I'm just listening and writing, listening and writing. My notes definitely get easier to decipher as the series goes on and the number of candidates reduces!

We'll speak to Alan and email him about 30 times throughout a task, I'd say. Issues like who has put themselves forward as project manager, who has declined (again) are important, as Alan crosschecks our information with their CVs. So if it's a market task and someone has worked on a stall, he'll want to ask why they didn't put themselves forward as project manager. Nothing passes him by. He would have made a fantastic QC: he can cross-examine anyone to get to the truth. Then, shortly before we go into the boardroom to face the candidates, we brief Alan further on what happened on the task, who did what, in a chronological and succinct way. There's no emotion, just facts: what happened on each task, who was team leader and how that came about, and who made which decisions.

It's quite a responsibility. That first series was particularly difficult for me because it coincided with selling Birmingham City. I was literally working 22 hours a day, and I was exhausted, but fortunately the club was sold part way through the filming so for the second half I didn't have to be up all night on the phone to the Far East. A lot of people said to me afterwards, 'You definitely looked better as the series went on.' Charming – but I thought, It's not surprising.

It's still a bit of a juggling act, though. Ideally, during the weeks of filming *The Apprentice*, I would just concentrate on that but, of course, I have to try to make it work alongside my role at West Ham. I shift the football working day to start at six p.m., and for a few weeks some of the staff have to work an evening shift. It's not ideal, and it's exhausting for me, but it's the only way to make it work.

It's the little things you don't think about that take up time. I still can't get my head around how many clothes I need when

I'm filming that show. I'm in London for 12 weeks and the weather can change entirely during that period. Then, some days you're in a market, some days you're on a hill, some days you're in a factory, some days you're in a shop, and the work involves a lot of standing and a lot of running around. I start each series with great intentions of having my outfits co-ordinated, getting my hair styled, and so on, and after about a day it's just too demanding to worry about. You can't think about how you look as well as listening and doing the job.

But if it's hard for us, it is harder for the candidates. *The Apprentice* illustrates very well how fine the line can be between enthusiasm and delusion – it's where much of the comedy comes from. The team's enthusiasm for an idea or approach can really mislead them. So, in my first series, the Apollo team came up with the Germinator, a cleaning spray, in the advertising task. They got this line into their heads, '*Hasta la vista, gravy*,' and built their entire campaign around it. Nobody said, 'Hang on a minute, this cleaning product doesn't clean gravy and it shouldn't be handled by children, but there's a child using it in our ad.' They allowed themselves to be carried away by that one idea. It's a rare person who will stand against the momentum and say, 'Let's have a think about the logic of this,' but often that person goes on to win.

And the lack of common sense can be shocking. There's the list task, where they've got one day to buy ten items and negotiate the prices. On the table there will be a bunch of directories for north London, central London, Greater London, the South-east and, of course, someone's looking in the north London book and someone else is looking at the South-east, and they just don't think laterally. Someone will say, 'We'll go here and get a light bulb, and then we'll go there and get a top hat.' I'm thinking, That journey will take you two hours each way. They say things like, 'I'll pop to Guildford.' And I'll be thinking, You'll *pop* to Guildford? No one 'pops' to Guildford. And then they'll go to London's Brick Lane, the well-known heart of Scotland, for Scottish tartan fabric!

It can be painful to watch them get it so wrong, and at the beginning I had a real urge to jump in and tell them. But, of course, Nick and I never intervene or give advice: that wouldn't be fair. Still, they'll be looking at us all the time, whenever they say anything, to gauge our reactions. Are we pulling faces? Was that a twitch of approval? But I can keep a straight face.

So, what makes a good candidate? Someone who has the measure of themselves, who understands what they're good at, who can take things in their stride, without getting overexcited and losing control. Someone who is over-ambitious can become too aggressive and lack patience – always a road to nowhere. Those candidates who are in control of themselves and offer a calm and thoughtful approach always do better. Those who put on an act never make it to the final stages. And those who are too self-focused are always brought into the boardroom for a grilling.

But we can't stand those who hide in the background: the stakes are too high to play games like that. Sit quietly, be anonymous and hope to sneak into the final stages? We can spot that approach miles away. Alan doesn't want to bring just anyone into his business or go into business with just anyone. Grounded, rounded and sensible are key factors. Understanding how to get the best out of people, not being afraid to get your hands dirty, taking care of the rubbish jobs and allowing someone else to take some of the glory are all important traits – as they are in business generally. And the nerve to take risks, even if they don't come off.

Ultimately, you need to get two kinds of strategy right to win. The first is for the task and the second is for the boardroom, which require different skill sets. In the tasks, you need to have ideas and articulate them; you should also be able to express clearly why you're not in favour of an idea or a strategy, rather than saying in an interview: 'I don't like this idea but I'm backing it.' That's arse-covering in case things go wrong. You should always be measured in your criticism – I hate people who criticise an idea but can't come up with an alternative. And, in the boardroom, be honest. Alan likes triers; he also likes people who can take responsibility when things go wrong. As long as you can explain your logic you may be forgiven.

If not, things can turn very quickly. I remember once we were in the boardroom with the final three candidates, who were so close to the prize. Normally, Alan doesn't let people speak when he does his summing up, but one candidate asked to say one more thing – and he let her. It was a mistake on her part: she disqualified herself by being rude about the other two candidates. Alan cannot bear disrespectful or rude people, and in seconds she went from being a strong contender to dismissal.

Of course, some aren't such a surprise. There are always one or two who can't contain themselves, and you know they won't last. But it's very tough for any of them to get it right: you need so many different aspects to your personality. You have to show that you can stand up for yourself when you need to, that when you have to work in a team you can, and that you understand the difference between a good idea and a bad one. The candidates must be confident and assertive enough to win each task, but they have to live in the shared house with their rivals and get on with them. If you're too confident, you'll trip up.

That is what happened to Melody Hossaini in the 2011 series. I really liked Melody, but she stood out as someone who was not enough of a team player. And no one had any idea what she did. Melody would talk about all these awards she'd won, and how Lord Sugar would be so proud of her, but that wasn't how it turned out. She'd say, 'I've won an award from the Dalai Lama and Al Gore.' So what did you do? 'Well, of course, after my award from Al Gore …' Okay, so what do you do? 'Well, I've got an award, I was personally taught by the Dalai Lama.' I still haven't a clue what she does.

I didn't guess that Tom Pellereau would win that year, but I think Alan's a great judge of character and it's good to see that genuinely nice guys can win. Helen Louise Milligan was a great candidate in that series, and had a job been on offer – rather than investment in a start-up business – I reckon she would have won hands down. But she's a corporate animal and her business idea showed that. What does she do? She's a PA. So what does she want to do as a business? Be a PA.

I really liked the 2010 winner, Stella English. She showed that she can think before she speaks, which is an exceptional quality on the show. Something just seems to happen to people during the filming of *The Apprentice*. There's a breakdown in engagement between the brain and the mouth, so the candidates start to say whatever comes into their head without thinking it through. I guess perhaps we all do it – maybe I just notice it more because I'm the one taking notes and listening. Susan Ma, in particular, in the 2011 series, offered some classics. When we were in Paris, she was selling child car seats and not getting very far, so she started coming out with things like, 'Do the French love their children?' and 'Do a lot of people drive in France?' She was very young and I think sometimes she just spoke her thoughts out loud. She is a great businesswoman and I suspect she will go a very long way in the future.

There are always some candidates you like more than others, but we're not with them long enough take a firm dislike to anyone. Some can be quite annoying – they get ridiculously excited: 'We're on a train, yeah!' And they all keep in touch, which is nice – a network of candidates, if you like.

Then there's the kids on the junior show, who are really impressive. Lord Sugar came up with *Junior Apprentice* – they've since changed the title to *Young Apprentice* – because he thinks teenagers get a really bad press and he wanted to show the other side to them. He wanted to show that being an entrepreneur is about working hard, taking risks and having energy, and the programme does just that. And you only have to watch the 2011 series to see how bloody marvellous the candidates were – some say they are far better collectively than many of the adults they've come across in the senior series – unbelievable, really.

For me, it's much harder not to get involved with the kids, and much harder to stop myself giving them advice on the tasks. And they're so desperate to talk to us because they think in some way that will help them. One will come up and say, 'I've got a sore throat,' then another says, 'I've got a bad cold.' I've got a teenager at home so I've seen all this before. I say, 'Is this the I-don't-want-to-go-to-school-today syndrome?' I tell them my own teenager pulls illness out of the air when things aren't going well, but you have to carry on, and if you don't you'll kick yourself. They all carry on. Although they'll still come up and ask me, 'Do you know any famous people?' and 'Have you met Lady Gaga?' Kids!

And while it's easy to be critical of the candidates when you're watching them on TV at home, you have to take your hat off to them. They are under so much pressure, and they're doing it week after week after week. It is really, really, really tough, and I know that better than anybody else – better than Nick and Alan, actually – because I was once a candidate myself. Back in 2007, before I had any involvement with the show, Alan asked me to do the first *Comic Relief Does The Apprentice*, the celebrity version for charity, and because he's a friend I said yes.

I had no idea what I was letting myself in for. The girls' team was going to be Jo Brand, Maureen Lipman, Trinny Woodall, Cheryl Cole and myself. The boys' team also promised to be an interesting mix – Alastair Campbell, Piers Morgan, Danny Baker, Rupert Everett and Ross Kemp.

The first morning in the boardroom, Alan gave a critique of everybody and, when he came to me, he said, 'You're the businesswoman among everybody here, so you have the most to lose reputation-wise.' And it suddenly dawned on me that, Oh, shit, yes, it was true. This wasn't just a bit of fun, it was going to be serious. A real spotlight turned on us – on me. I left the boardroom thinking, Oh, my God, what have I done?

But Rupert Everett was like a rabbit in the headlights, asking, 'Where's my script?' I said, 'There is no script. It's reality and it's live.' As an actor used to learning his lines, he was terrified. 'I can't work without a script!' And more was in store for poor Rupert.

When I saw Piers the next morning he had a story to tell: 'Oh my God, Alastair told Rupert to ring up Madonna to get some money off her because, apparently, they're good friends, and Rupert said, "You don't ring Madonna, you have to write her a letter."' Soon after that, Rupert walked out of the show. I said he should have come on the girls' team – he would have been happier with us!

Meanwhile, as soon as we had returned to our base – a suite at the Mayfair Hotel – the girls' team chose me to be the project manager. I had to be completely organised: finding something for everybody to do that they felt comfortable with, making sure those strong personalities pulled together and that we won. The winner would be the team that raised the most money for charity, so my focus was entirely on that.

The task was to organise a celebrity funfair, so there was lots of negotiating over which team got the best rides, and so on, but I said to my girls, 'Look, we'll win this by raising the most money on ticket sales, and most of that will come from the tickets you sell beforehand. It doesn't matter how good or bad the fairground rides are – that's just a distraction. We'll win or lose this before we even get there.' That's basic business sense – make sure you know which race you're in.

So, I made sure that selling tickets was our focus, but one of the huge pressures of *The Apprentice* is that there is so much else that has to get done too. In the tasks, there are always the glamorous jobs and the shit jobs, and I was involved in all the shit jobs. Like spending half the day with Jo and Maureen cleaning mountains of squid to serve at the funfair, with the ink popping in my eyes.

Trinny and Cheryl, meanwhile, were on the phone selling tickets, and I remember Trinny saying, 'I know about this party tonight that we have to go to – there will be lots of famous people who we might get to buy tickets.' So off she went home to get changed, while I went straight to the party from the squid cleaning. It was awful. I showed up at this beautiful house, this beautiful party, full of politicians, pop stars, celebrities, and I had no make-up on, I looked terrible, and I probably smelled of squid.

But then I walked in and there was Sir Philip Green. Now, Piers is a friend, so I'd been chatting to him, and he'd been banging on all day that he'd got the Topshop owner on his side. My team been selling tickets hard, and I knew we'd done well – we'd got £100,000 out of Littlewoods and a couple of hundred grand out of other people – but Sir Philip is generous and will donate whatever he likes. If he was supporting the boys, I could have no idea whether we were ahead.

There was only one thing to do, stinking of squid or not. Philip was standing on the landing when I wriggled through the crowd. 'Philip, why are you going with Piers? Most of your retail outlets are for women, so you should be supporting the women's team.' And so I swung him from the boys to the girls. He didn't leave them high and dry – the boys got products for their stall from his stores – but we got hard cash. He was amazing to us and to the Comic Relief charity, donating an enormous sum. You've got to take your chances where you can!

That wasn't the only time Piers was useful to me because he can't keep his mouth shut. I'd say, in a very innocent way, 'What are you up to?' and he'd reply, 'I'm in at Goldman Sachs!' or wherever he was. So I'd get on the phone to a friend and ask him if he knew anyone at that bank. It turned out he knew the chairman in the London office, and gave me his number. When I rang the Goldman chairman and asked if he was doing anything with Piers, he said he hadn't decided. 'You must do it with us ladies. We're definitely going to win. We've got the support of Philip Green,' I said.

He said, 'All right then,' and gave us £25,000. Bingo.

Part of it was knowing how to get people to do what you want them to do. Piers's strategy was to force people to donate – to say, 'If you don't give me any money I'm going to tell the world that you haven't given me any money.' But, of course, most people don't want to be bullied into donating to charity – or to be bullied into doing anything. I took a different approach. To persuade Philip, I'd said: 'If you give us £100,000, we'll do the following for you. I'll be your chauffeur for a day. Maureen Lipman will be your Jewish mother for the day. Jo Brand will come to your office and tell you jokes. Trinny will take you on a shopping trip and Cheryl will be your secretary.' We even wrote an IOU, although we haven't done it yet! But it was a bit of a joke, a bit of fun – and people respond to that.

Piers could cope with it – he's seen his share of rough and tumble, having been a tabloid-newspaper editor. But emotions ran high. At one point, Cheryl actually said to me, 'Don't leave me with Trinny because I'm going to kill her.' And Maureen and Trinny had a huge fall-out. The problem was that we had a limited number of tickets to sell, and Maureen had a friend who was prepared to pay £25 to come. But Trinny said, 'She can't have one for that.' Obviously, every ticket had to pay, but people had to be included, too. I said to them both: 'Listen, we never have to see each other after this, but for the next two days, just focus – it's not asking much, and it's for charity.' And they did. I worked it so that they both had their way – I got more tickets!

On another occasion, the boys kidnapped our chef. It was a bit of fun, really, but Trinny went down to their room and got worked up. Alastair – I didn't know him before the show but I liked him – phoned me and said, 'It's all gone off,' then Piers phoned me and said, 'Trinny's crying.' So I turned up and calmed things down a bit.

Trinny – best known for her show *What Not To Wear* – was an interesting character to work with. She's very competitive and always 'up' – always bang, bang, bang, bang – but very controlled at the same time. I remember, at the end of it all, she said to me, 'I just want to say well done, because I know I'm very difficult and you handled me very well.' And I do have a talent for dealing with difficult people. I think the ability to manage people – to have a sort of sixth sense of what they want to achieve from something – is instinctive. It isn't something you can always teach. In that situation, I made sure Trinny had plenty to do, that she was always praised and felt she'd got the spotlight. She was happy, so we were happy. And they were all great in the end. Everyone contributed, and it was a real team effort.

Still, I lost about a stone in three days. There was just so much to do. I was out selling, controlling Trinny and getting the best out of Cheryl – persuading her to call showbiz types like Louis Walsh and Simon Cowell and ask them buy tickets, which they did – and helping Jo and Maureen do all the food. Not only was I doing all this graft, but I was up until two o'clock in the morning, planning everything and making sure we'd followed all the rules, which were quite complicated. For instance, there was a rule that we couldn't just get someone to pledge money: they had to come to the event in person. So it wasn't just about getting a donation from someone like Simon Cowell, we had to make sure he turned up – which is trickier. But Cheryl did that. She was fantastic.

Things went wrong all the time. We'd ordered megaphones and, when we got to the fairground, we realised they were all still in the boxes, needing to be assembled. We had to get them out, bit by bit, and put them together. It was a laborious task and took ages. I was sitting on the floor, thinking, Oh, my God, but you just have to get on with it. But there were funny moments, too. When Geri Halliwell came to help us sell raffle tickets, Trinny was giving her these complicated instructions, and Geri just looked at her and said, 'Trinny, I know how to sell a raffle ticket.' And there was so much goodwill. It was a lovely once-in-a-lifetime experience.

It was a fun challenge for me: I had to look at every which way we could raise the most money. For example, there was a £100,000 bonus for whoever took the most money on the food at their fairground and I was determined to get it. I told my girls we'd make the rides free when someone bought food, so that way all the donations we raked in counted as spending on food. I got £17,000 for one glass of champagne that night, and £20,000 for a bowl of my squid! So, of course, we won the bonus. When Alastair Campbell found out, he phoned me and said, 'You jammy bastard – that was genius.' It was great.

By the time we got to the boardroom I was pretty sure we'd won – but, you never know. Then, when they read the results out, we had made £774,000 and the boys £286,000. We'd done it! We'd won. And poor Piers got fired! When the programme came out, Jo Brand – who was brilliant, a real grafter – told me that, when her husband saw it, he said, 'You're not in it at all – were you lying when you said you were?' Not everyone got an equal showing, that's for sure. But it was a lot of fun.

So, I've done it myself, and having done it myself, I can see why *The Apprentice* can create a sort of madness because you're trying to do so many things under so much time pressure. You're trying to manage five people; everyone wants their say and to put their ideas; they want to debate everything, but you can't allow that because you haven't got time. It needs real clarity of thought, real division of labour and, above all, perhaps, hard graft. And I couldn't have done it if I hadn't been team leader. It would have been a total nightmare!

How can you exhibit some of that *Apprentice* spirit yourself? It's never too early. Follow some true *Apprentice* advice. If you're still at school, get your birthday money, then go to a wholesaler and buy some goods. Sell them in the market. Use the money to restock and sell again. Smell the winners and dump the losers: that's the idea that Alan started with, and he even has a task like that in the series. To be an Apprentice, you need determination, enthusiasm and energy. You need spirit more than a qualification, and that's the lesson Alan teaches everyone throughout this show.

In the end, it's just like business. Take a risk on yourself, push yourself, follow a dream, work hard and keep going – that's the message.

CH.11
DID SOMEONE SAY THE F-WORD?

'I only know that people call me a feminist whenever I express sentiments that differentiate me from a doormat.' I love that quote, from the writer Rebecca West. I've never played the gender game. I've never been a 'You said that because I'm a woman' type. But I do believe in certain things and I talk publicly about them.

The term 'feminist' is almost a dirty word nowadays – I hate that. It conjures up thoughts of bra-burners and man-haters, has been hijacked by stereotypes and has lost its meaning. I'd like to be able to take it back and show people its true meaning – which I believe is 'an advocate of women's rights', in relation to our political, social and economic equality to men. It's the twenty-first century and still, in many cases, more than we'll ever know, men are paid more than women for the same job. That's not right. If women like me won't stand up for our rights, then who will?

So, when Richard Keys and Andy Gray, the Sky Sports presenters, were recorded talking disparagingly about the female linesman Sian Massey, suggesting that she couldn't do her job because she was a woman, I stuck my neck out, said what I thought and found myself at the centre of the row that resulted in both men losing their jobs.

I could have drawn down the blinds and said nothing. I think many people would have done exactly that – it would have been easier and more comfortable. But it would have been wrong, because this was a monumentally significant moment. It's not what Keys and Gray said that was so important – we all know what sexism is. What was significant for me was the outcome. Because in the same way that, a few years ago, the ITV pundit Ron Atkinson had to resign after he used a racist word when he thought he was off camera, the Keys and Gray incident showed that sexism is as unacceptable as racism. To say that a woman is not capable of doing a job purely on the basis of her gender is not acceptable. It is unacceptable to say so and, more importantly, it's wrong to think so.

We were then in the middle of a tough season at West Ham, and I had been having a hard time with the press, particularly the *Mirror*. The paper had published inaccurate reports – which they later apologised for and paid me libel damages for – that I had been texting the players to get them to 'rise up' against our then manager, Avram Grant. Meanwhile other papers were spreading rumours that Paul and I had separated. That

Saturday, 22 January 2011, I wrote in my *Sun* column that, for the first time in my life, I was 'experiencing sexism at its rankest, lies about my personal life and a level of calculated mischief that is simply appalling'.

That night I had a phone call from the *Mail on Sunday*, asking what I thought of Richard Keys and Andy Gray's remarks about me. I had no idea what they were talking about, so they told me: earlier that day the two Sky Sports presenters had been recorded talking, while they thought their microphones were turned off, and Keys had made a comment about my column: 'Did you hear charming Karren Brady this morning complaining about sexism? Do me a favour, love.'

On the face of it, it didn't seem particularly offensive, so I asked the paper what sort of reaction they were expecting from me. They said they thought it was sexist, but I said I needed to hear it in context and that I wasn't prepared to comment until I had. I'm used to getting calls from the press and, to be honest, I thought it was a little story that would go away. But, the next morning, when the *Mail on Sunday* broke the story, it was suddenly everywhere. Along with everyone else, I read the full transcript of what Keys and Gray had said, and again I decided to say nothing. But, later in the day, Victoria Derbyshire from *Five Live* phoned me.

I really like Victoria, so I decided to talk to her about what had gone on. I still hadn't heard the tape of the conversation so I hadn't heard the tone or the way it was said until Victoria played it to me, off air. And it was only then that I realised how shocking it was. You could hear the venom in their voices – it was really nasty, really vicious. Here's some of what they said, but I do think you need to hear it to get the full impact:

KEYS: Somebody better get down there and explain offside to her [Sian].

GRAY: Can you believe that? A female linesman. Women don't know the offside rule.

KEYS: 'Course they don't. I guarantee there'll be a big one today. Kenny [Dalgliesh, Liverpool manager] will go potty. This is not the first time, is it? Didn't we have one before? Wendy Toms? ... The game's gone mad.

'My blood is literally boiling,' I told Victoria. I was outraged, and so disappointed. All the time, you think you're making progress in championing women in your industry, but the reality is that you're not because of dinosaurs like Richard Keys. He was the main offender, I thought. If you listen, Andy Gray was mostly saying, 'Yeah, yeah,' but with Keys there was this real venom, this real anti-women sentiment. It was really, really sexist.

I didn't much care about what they'd said about me, that was nothing, but I felt for Sian. I'm sure it's hard enough dealing with the players and the crowd, the pressure of doing her job – I understand that feeling – without having Richard Keys saying things like that before the match had even started.

So I found myself faced with the big question: would I stand up and say what I thought publicly? Sian, I knew, was not allowed to speak because of the terms of her contract with the FA. I didn't want to get involved, but if I said nothing, no one would say anything, and nothing would happen. Nothing would change for my daughter, or my daughter's daughter.

It was one of those times in life when I could have said, 'This has nothing to do with me,' and I'm pretty sure that's what a lot of people would have done. But someone had to say, 'No, it's not good enough and it's not right and I'm not going to tolerate my daughter hearing this and never thinking about football as a career option.' When Victoria asked me if I would go on air, I said yes.

There were three reasons why I was so unhappy. First was the obvious point that you can't judge someone's ability before you've seen what they can do. The match hadn't even begun and those two men had made a decision that Sian could not be an effective linesman, for no reason other than her gender. I'd truly thought that style of thinking had gone, the 'I won't get on an aeroplane if it's a female pilot' style of thinking. On top of that, how could anybody who has influence as a broadcaster not be politically aware enough to know that even if you think it you shouldn't say it?

The second reason I was unhappy was the hypocrisy. Those two men only had the conversation they had because they thought they were off air. They would never have said those things for broadcast or to her face or mine. They talked to each other in that way like mates – but when the shit hit the fan, they couldn't stand up and say, 'Yeah, that's what we believe.' Of course they couldn't. And once it was exposed, they were contrite – so hypocritical. I was shocked that the public persona could be so different from the private person. The way I saw it was that Andy Gray is who he is, and doesn't pretend to be anyone else, but Richard Keys portrays himself differently. But this one instant told us all we needed to know about his true attitudes.

The third and most important thing for me was the possible consequences. As somebody who runs businesses and works in the media, I was very interested to see what Sky Sports were going to do about their two presenters. The station's actions were critical because its management's reaction would show whether this was or wasn't seen as an important issue. Were they going to stand up and say, as part of a major organisation with shareholders, that, actually, no, this is not right and, no, we're not going to accept it? Or were they going to try and push it under the carpet and hope it went away? Because in the immediate aftermath it did seem possible that Keys and Gray could get away with it.

So on Five Live I spoke out: 'I just think it's unfair. Here is somebody doing a very important job under very difficult circumstances, who deserves and warrants our respect, and here are two people, who other people listen to and get their views from, not giving her a chance.

'Everyone is entitled to a personal opinion, but what really upsets me is the fact that only females in our industry are judged by their gender and that is categorically wrong.'

I said that I felt the comments were deeply sexist. 'You know, "We'd better go down and tell her the offside rule." I'm surprised they didn't say, "We'd better go down and tell her to put the kettle on."'

And I said how disappointed I was. 'It never would have occurred to me that they had those views, whether public or private. It almost makes it worse that they're speaking when the microphones are not on, as opposed to when they are on, because they don't have the brass neck to say it publicly; they would only say it privately.'

I was trying to place an onus on Sky to respond. I wanted to make the point that many other women out there were trying to carve out a career and that we didn't think it was right that we were prejudged on our ability, based on our gender. So I made the point that it would be very interesting to see how seriously Sky took this issue. That the ball was in their court to decide if they agreed with me – or whether it was a case of all-the-lads-together and it was just a big laugh.

The story just got bigger and bigger and bigger. Other stuff started coming out – these things are like a rolling stone. Clips were posted on YouTube, including one that showed Andy Gray being suggestive to a female Sky presenter, Charlotte Jackson. At that point Sky stepped up and Gray was fired.

That left Richard Keys under pressure. On the Wednesday he came out and said he had tried to ring me a couple of times on the Sunday to apologise but I hadn't answered my phone. That infuriated me. As if somehow it was my fault because I hadn't taken his call. I was being criticised because I hadn't taken his call so that he could apologise? I hadn't asked to be involved in this. I hadn't asked him to say those things about Sian or about me.

It annoyed me so much, the assumption that if Richard Keys said, 'Oh, I'm sorry, dear,' it would make it all right, because he had been prepared to do me the great honour of ringing me up. As if he was up there and I was down here, waiting for his gracious apology. It was a great insight into the way he saw things. Plus, he implied that I would be pleased that the scandal had taken the attention off West Ham.

My response was to fight fire with fire, which is typical of me – I replied via the media:

Perhaps Richard thought I was too busy making the tea and washing up to take his call, but a cursory glance at the weekend's newspapers or television would have made him well aware that I was heavily occupied with the West Ham and Newham Council Olympic Stadium bid.

West Ham's future in the Olympic Stadium is of far more importance to me than his future.

It is most unfortunate that he has chosen to add insult to

injury by suggesting that he has done me a favour by getting West Ham out of the press as, after all, I did not ask to be part of his sexist tirade.

This is not about an apology to me, but about an apology to all women. Richard represents views that myself and those who work in the business of football find totally dinosaur.

Richard Keys resigned that night.

I think Sky had taken a really big leap of faith in doing the right thing. Keys and Gray were very popular – they had the big shows and a great following. Sky could have tried to fudge some sort of apology and hope the situation would go away, but they didn't do that. They made it clear that sexism was unacceptable. And as a result a marker was put down: that women will stand up for themselves and won't let people make 'jokes' like that, because such attitudes are not OK.

I got lots of support, which was good, but I'm not the sort of person who needs support. I knew I was doing the right thing. In fact, I didn't speak to Sian at any stage, and we have never spoken about it since. I didn't want anyone to think it was 'all the ladies' together. I knew that would be the next accusation – that we'd got together over our cauldron and brewed up some 'Let's get people sacked' plan. But it wasn't me who lost Richard Keys his job. He did that himself. Looking back, I still think everything about that incident was revolting.

Yet it didn't leave me wondering whether more men in football are secretly thinking such things, because I don't think they are. In the boardroom there's none of that sexism. You wouldn't hear any chief execs or chairmen of football clubs speaking like that, and I don't think that sort of thinking is rife on the terraces either. But it did make me realise that some people in the sports media are really anti-women. The bottom line is that some journalists, or pundits, just don't believe there's a place in sport for women. They think it's a man's game and that's that.

The problem is, I think, that they can get stuck in this old-fashioned idea of how life is. And I also think that sometimes people who work in that environment are pampered and protected when they're at the top of their profession. They develop a sense of huge authority and find it very difficult when they've made an error. They don't know what to do.

I have no regrets. I'm glad I spoke out, and I think the whole thing will have shone a spotlight on the attitudes of people in the public eye and the respect they accord their female colleagues. The overwhelming response to Keys and Gray's comments, and Sky's actions, has made entirely clear that it is not fair or appropriate to judge someone by gender before you've seen the quality of their work. I am proud to have helped to make that happen.

Of course, it was one small battle in a much bigger fight. There are many women all over the world who struggle to get an education, a job, to have the basic advantage of freedom of choice. Women who will never know independence. Women for whom a man, a male relative, will decide who and when they will marry. Women who, due to where they are born and where they live, are still walking two paces behind a man.

That's why many people believe that gender inequality is the biggest moral challenge of our age, and I agree 100 per cent. There are still many countries in the world where women are not allowed to own their own property or inherit from their fathers, where they are denied the right to work and the right to proper health care. To make progress, we have to ensure that the barriers to women's independence and freedom of choice, whether these be laws, customs or environment, are pulled down and that women enjoy access to health, services, education, political positions, employment and, most importantly, opportunity across the world.

Even though it may seem that there is graver injustice or more damaging inequality abroad, that does not mean we can rest on our laurels at home. There are many companies in this country where women do most of the work, but men make most of the decisions. Even in industries where women are well represented, be it caring or administration, they are still not making it to the top management level in sufficient numbers. Far too few women make up the boards of our public companies.

That's why I will not invest a single penny in any company that does not have women on its board of directors. While I don't believe in forcing companies to appoint women, I do believe that every company that does not have women on its board should tell its shareholders and stakeholders why not, and what they have done to try to address it. How many women have they interviewed? What missing skills have meant that these women were not appointed? Then we would learn more about what to teach our girls and more about the barriers – and excuses – blocking women's progress.

In my experience, the best companies in the world are mixed and diverse, not full of people in the same mould with the same education and background, all too busy patting themselves on the back as they fall off the side of the cliff. For the same reason, the best company boards represent a wide and diverse mix of people – including those who are not afraid to offer a fresh perspective and ask why – why is this important to our company? People who will question if the decisions made at the highest level are truly in the best interests of the company, the customers, shareholders and staff, people who are not afraid to say, 'This is not what we stand for, we do not agree.'

Ultimately, my strategy is to encourage more women into business, to encourage more women into traditionally male-dominated industries and to ensure that women are treated equally. One way in which I can effect change is to use my profile to climb over barriers, campaign and raise awareness. I can also encourage our politicians and businesspeople to address these issues. I want to believe that, in the future, opportunities in whatever field, in whatever circumstances, will be equal. As I write, three women, Ellen Johnson Sirleaf, Leymah Gbowee and Tawakkol Karman, have just shared the Nobel Peace Prize 2011 'for their non-violent struggle for the safety of women and for women's rights to full participation in peace-building work'. Three amazing women, who keep fighting and ensuring that these issues are always at the front of people's minds. So I do have hope.

And, if you are the first woman anything, and I'm told I'm the first woman in football, then that's something to take heart from – because you have opened a door. The trick is to hold that door open as wide as possible, for as long as possible, to allow other women to march through it. I can say, with my hand on my heart, that I have tried to do that. Three-quarters of my senior management team at Birmingham City FC were women. And I have so far appointed three senior people to West Ham's executive board, and they are all women. Because if I don't do it, then who will?

CH.12
NO TIME TO SLOW DOWN
MY CAREER TODAY

Now that my thoughts are turning to how I can help other women succeed, does that mean I am approaching my own time to slow down, to kick back, to enjoy the fruits of my labours? You might well ask, but in a word, no. I just don't want to.

One of the things that has helped me throughout my career is that, for me, there's not a massive divide between work and play. At my core, I love business, it is my hobby as well as my job, and I would rather spend a day at Mothercare or at Channel 4 than I would playing tennis or shopping. I like structure. Maybe that is a bit sad, but the truth is that I would much rather go to a series of meetings than a spa day! And that's why much of what you might call my spare time is nowadays spent on the boards of various companies, in addition to my 'day job' at West Ham.

It all started in 2003, when I was contacted by a headhunter about becoming a non-executive director with Moss Bros, the men's clothing store. As I often do, I talked it over with David Sullivan, and he thought it was a good idea, but in the end I decided that one wasn't for me. I like retail – it's competitive, direct and tangible – but Moss Bros was small and I didn't have any real interest in the business. But it had piqued my interest. When the same role at Mothercare came up, I thought it would be a good fit. Sophia and Paolo were younger then, so I was a Mothercare customer myself.

There were four interviews, which was strange for me, because of course I hadn't been interviewed for a job for years. The process is that first you meet the headhunter, then, if he likes you, you go forward to meet the chairman, then the chief executive, and then the senior non-executive – that's the most senior person on the board next to the chairman – and, finally, I was approved. Soon afterwards, the same headhunter contacted me about being a non-executive director at Channel 4. Again, I thought that would be a great fit for me. I have experienced the media from all sides – both as the subject of reporters' interest and also appearing on screen in a variety of television shows and writing my own columns for various publications and newspapers.

Channel 4 was a whole different ballgame. As a public-service broadcaster, it represented my first experience of working in a taxpayer-owned organisation – albeit one that doesn't get public money but is instead a commercial operation. I turned up for the preliminary meeting with Luke Johnson, who had recently taken over as chairman, expecting the process to be the same as at Mothercare, but instead of just sitting down with Luke there was a panel waiting for me, including someone from Ofcom, the industry regulator, and a government observer. At Mothercare, the interviews had been pretty formulaic, all about business process and risk strategy, but this was totally different, all about my personal opinions and views, what I thought about swearing on TV, and the like.

Afterwards, I phoned Paul and told him I didn't think I was going to get it. One of the questions they had asked me was: 'You seem very busy, are you sure you really want to do it?' – which didn't fill me with optimism. On top of that, if joining Mothercare had involved four interviews, I imagined this time around it would be more like 15, what with all the different government hoops you have to leap through. But then, as we were talking, my mobile rang. It was Luke Johnson. 'Fantastic,' he said. 'When can you start?'

When I rang Paul back and said, 'Actually, I got it,' he said he knew I would – he has that faith in me. I remember being so happy, at both appointments – although I'm not quite sure I knew what I was letting myself in for. The key thing about being a non-exec of a company is to remember you are not the CEO. In a nutshell, non-execs are responsible for the work the company's executives do and ensuring that they do it professionally and correctly. As members of the board, you are there to assess the strategy of the company, the risks, the branding, the ideas. Basically, you are making sure that the company deals with its shareholders in an appropriate way, and that it is doing things professionally and properly.

It is a huge responsibility and you don't get rich being a non-exec, so it is really important that you choose positions that you are interested in. People say it is only 12 days of work a year, but there is a vast amount of reading and background work involved. You are not going to be able to assess the health of a company just by attending one meeting every couple of months – you have to spend time with the executives, you have to be bothered to delve into the figures, you have to be interested in the process.

The new generation of non-execs is far more involved in the business than the old school, where you would have a nice little lunch and a brandy and toddle off home, or however they used to do it. Nowadays it is bloody hard work – but so interesting. What really appeals to me is the variety. If you are in one business for too long you can become very closeted, and particularly with football, I think. When you are paying people £20,000 a week, you can lose touch with what the real world is all about, and I think a lot of football people are guilty of that. That's definitely not something that you risk working in retail, where it's all about your customers, the paying public.

I was really keen to get the chance to look into the books of one of Britain's strongest retail brands, Mothercare. It has an incredible pull, with around four in five pregnant mothers heading through its doors. But when I joined its board it was in a complete state, with all sorts of problems, both logistically and in terms of cash flow. You would go into a Mothercare shop for a pushchair and find it was out of stock, and the staff would know they had one somewhere in the company, but couldn't tell you where. And, actually, because people really liked the brand they *would* go back and try again, but it would likely be another no. Mothercare was trading on its brand, not on its product – on its reputation rather than the reality.

Ben Gordon was brought in as CEO just before I joined and I heard that cash flow was so bad, he even took the floats out of the tills to keep the company functioning. But these are the challenges that make business so exciting. It must be quite a different sort of experience to go on to the board of an organisation that is steady as she goes. Some of the boards I have been on have faced real issues that needed a speedy resolution where it was a case of all hands on deck – hard work, but great fun.

As ever, what most interested me with Mothercare was the brand and marketing. I wanted to look at what would differentiate it from being just a run-of-the-mill shop and mark it out as a champion for good parenting. So, I encouraged staff training, because if you go into Mothercare and say, 'My baby has got colic, what should I do?' you expect staff to have the answer.

Or, 'I have got a six-month-old baby, when should I take him out of the pushchair and put him in a pram?' 'What nappies do I need?' When people come to Mothercare, they are not walking into a shed full of stuff like in a big supermarket, they are walking into what they consider to be a specialist retailer. We needed to up our game to match those expectations – as every good business must do.

I was also concerned about the compliance side of things: making sure your business is sticking to the rules and maintaining high standards. I remembered this big story breaking about a football club whose shirts were being made in a sweatshop, and I could just see what a nightmare it would be in terms of brand damage if this happened to a baby-focused retailer. Imagine the fallout if it emerged that child labourers had been involved somewhere down the production line for products for children! I wanted to ensure we had all the right checks in the factories so we could genuinely put our hands on our hearts and say, 'We have done everything that is physically possible in this area.' That was very important to me. And we did achieve that.

Another important role for non-execs is when tough decisions have to be made, I realised. Sometimes you need to have someone say, 'Hang on a minute, this is OK.' Pay is a classic example – people can get very scared when the spotlight falls on what you are doling out to your highest earners. The chairman of the remuneration committee at Mothercare had put together a scheme that was very tough, but that did pay out when execs hit their targets, and it paid out to the tune of millions of pounds. Then of course there's a panic that in this tough economic climate, executives were going to earn millions.

But I supported it. You need to stand up and say, 'Look, we should be thrilled to be paying this because it means that the company has done well.' Rather than be embarrassed, we should be saying: 'We brought in a CEO who has done the most fantastic job, who has created dividends and wealth for all the shareholders, and it is right and proper that he should be paid what was predetermined.' But people are afraid of the headlines.

I saw the same nerves at Channel 4, a public body where somebody could earn more than the Prime Minister. Well, yes, but if that person left to go to a fully commercial broadcaster such as ITV they would add a nought on to the end of their pay checque. Without paying market rates – or close to them – we wouldn't boast the talented people that we have.

But that would be far from the biggest challenge we faced there. I'll never forget the Shilpa Shetty racism row in 2007, over the Bollywood star's treatment by her fellow contestants on *Big Brother*. We were all door-stopped by journalists and there was a general cry of: 'What are you going to do about this?'

It was interesting – I won't say pleasant! – to witness a situation like that from the inside. As I always say, what marks out great leaders is what you do when you don't know what to do. This situation was a classic example. Lots of people love the kudos of running a company when things are going well, but it is quite a different kettle of fish when things are not going well. They can face personal criticism to an extent they have never experienced before. And, at Channel 4, it was felt that the chief executive Andy Duncan sort of disappeared from the scene as the organisation came under attack, and Luke Johnson as chairman had to come out and speak on behalf of the company.

That wasn't right, I thought. When you are running a team of people faced with a big problem, you have got to be the first person to stand up and say, 'Look, this is what has happened and this is the mistake that has been made, this is how it is going to be rectified, this is what we believe in, this is what we stand for, and this is what we are going to do.' If you don't get that right, you have an even bigger problem on your hands. It is understandable that people are scared – 'There is someone outside my house!' – but, ultimately, you have to shrug it off. After all, I have people outside my house all the time.

I think, at Channel 4, in that situation, the real issue was fear. Some executives didn't know what to say and didn't want the spotlight to fall on them, I felt. Yes, the Shilpa Shetty situation was a difficult and sensitive one to handle, but there has to be some perspective on these things, and it is the CEO's job to bring that. The worst thing you can do is go running, because the media only comes running after you – as became very clear.

The situation turned into something out of a comedy. At one point we were in the boardroom, hiding – the room was literally blacked out, with stuff all over the windows so people couldn't get a view. I had never seen anything like it. I remember saying: 'Rather than thinking about what we should say, what has actually happened? What is actually our view and what are we actually going to do about it?' I asked Kevin Lygo, who was head of TV, to tell us what he thought, and he articulated a position in three minutes. I said, 'That is what we should be standing up and saying.' So then Luke was given a few lines to go outside and read to the waiting press. Our position was that we abhorred racism, took our audience's worries seriously and were reviewing the programme. So we were laying our cards on the table, not hiding away.

The major decision that we had to make was whether to keep *Big Brother* or whether the show had had its day. Should we let it go? Around that time, Channel 4 was looking for a public subsidy to help it adapt to a digital era. Channel 4 is the fourth channel under the traditional, analogue set-up, but in a digital world it is one among hundreds – far greater competition. That did not make the situation any easier. Here we were, saying that we were a public body for public broadcasting, and people would reply: 'Yes, but what about *Big Brother* ...' The question being, how did that sort of show square with that public-service ethos?

But *Big Brother* made up around a quarter of Channel 4's total viewing figures at the time. It was the commercial vehicle that generated much of the revenue which allowed us to put on all the incredibly powerful, award-winning and – crucially – expensive documentaries that Channel 4 is famous for. If you just do those sorts of programmes and don't have that commercial element, whether it be in the form of *Big Brother* or shows like *Desperate Housewives*, you become BBC2. And the licence fee means that the BBC just isn't under the same pressure to make money as Channel is. Channel 4 is a real sort of Jekyll and Hyde business: it's a not-for-profit organisation that relies on commercial income. It cannot make any of its own shows, due to its public remit, but it has to generate enough money to buy the shows that make it competitive in a commercial market. So it was always about finding that difficult and politically charged balance between what is generating revenue and what is public-service broadcasting.

I supported ending *Big Brother*. It was time for a change, I thought. The show was a huge revenue generator but it had also become a huge liability. It was incredibly expensive, the audience was slowly dipping away, and the cost of the contract renewal with the production company, Endemol, was a king's ransom. My view was: what else can we put in that timeslot, that may not generate as many viewers, but could breathe new life into the channel and build a new body of viewers? I thought that there was probably still some life left in *Big Brother* but in a different concept, in a different way, but because of the cost of the Endemol contract, you had to be committed to it. I would have liked to keep the *Celebrity Big Brother* format only.

The upshot was that *Big Brother* was dropped from the channel, as I envisaged, and sold to Channel 5, so Richard Desmond now runs it. While it is not as successful as it once was, it takes up a lot of broadcast time and produces some headlines for his newspapers alongside. So good for him.

Ultimately, I like to think I brought more of a business focus to Channel 4, helping to create a bit of energy in the room. When I first went there, people were half asleep. In fact, I won't name names, but one person literally was asleep! Luke Johnson had a really big job to do to change the board and bring in professional, focused people who could and would make a contribution and help him bring the business into the twenty-first century. And I took it very seriously. At the time, there were a couple of leaks from the Channel 4 board and I remember Luke saying to me: 'The only person I would put my life on never saying anything is you.' I think he knew who was doing it anyway, but any of my own non-execs would say the same thing. I have got enough problems of my own without creating any more.

All in all, it was a very interesting seven years for me, and I can look back on it with pride. Luke changed Channel 4 for the better, with decisions like cutting ties with *Big Brother* and making the film *Slumdog Millionaire*, which won eight Oscars.

And these things were set out under a strategy devised during my time on the board. But you are allowed only a fixed time as a non-exec at the channel, and I'd stayed the full stretch.

My time at Mothercare, too, I look back on with warmth. I was there from 2003 till 2010, and it was great. I still meet up with people I worked alongside and feel good about what we achieved. Some people on the board, past and present, have said to me, 'You cut through the crap, you made decisions, you pushed people along. There are always people on the board that want to hide back behind other people – you clearly identified what some of the issues were.' And I am sure that this is a complete coincidence, but since I left Mothercare the share price has gone down the toilet!

But still, seven years is a long time and in the end I resigned to become a non-exec with Arcadia, Sir Philip Green's fashion retail group. I wanted to stay in retail but work with an owner, a driver of the business, who was far more entrepreneurial. I had met Philip a number of times and I thought of him as a businessman who thinks outside the box, who can discuss all sorts of topics across a wide range, as opposed to just having a narrower retail focus.

Topshop, Miss Selfridge and Dorothy Perkins are just some of the fantastic brands under his Arcadia umbrella, and again it was a business that employs lots of women, which I like. But what also appealed to me – and what appealed to me the most – was the opportunity to work with Philip. And having joined him to become a non-exec with Arcadia I have not been disappointed. I have been excited about what I found and what I have learnt from him.

He is without doubt the most dynamic, the most energetic, the most relentless businessperson I have ever come across, a whirlwind of energy and ideas. I have never met anyone quite like him. In fact, if you travelled to the deepest south or the furthest north you would never meet anyone like him. More importantly, he is a great mentor to all the people in his organisation and enjoys engaging with people at every level of the business. He is available 24/7 and his is one of the few mobile phones that is answered any time of the day or night.

He is at his best when there is a problem – which might be incredibly complicated with lots of financial detail, but he has the ability to cut straight through it and find the solution. He has such a fantastic instinct for knowing what the right thing to do is and, if you leave him to resolve it, it will be resolved.

Philip is happy to turn adviser and often does, whatever the circumstances. He is a good friend to people. I know that if you have him as a supporter in tough moments you'll not go wrong. Many different people, across many different types of businesses, have found this, and the help and support that he gives is not about financial gain. It is not about money, it is about getting things right and wanting to help others to get things right.

He also builds great teams of people. With Ian Grabiner, his CEO at Arcadia, you have a perfect match of people with complementary skills, running a fantastic business employing over 44 thousand people.

As I write, I have been on his board for over a year and during that time have been in some pretty intensive meetings with him that can last over a number of hours, even days. He holds a room with his energy and his ability to communicate. To put together a deal is an art and in Philip I have not found anyone better.

But it is not all about sitting on other people's boards; I have my own businesses too. I am a professional speaker, and often give talks at conferences and dinners. Public speaking doesn't faze me, in fact I enjoy it. I was always good at debating at school and in the years since I think I can say I have perfected the craft! For instance, when we wanted to buy West Ham we faced a lot of competition and had to do a presentation to the banks who had taken control of the business, as the previous owners had gone into liquidation. So David Sullivan and I turned up in a room full of 25 bankers, where I talked the talk. And we got the club.

Jo Malone, who created the perfume brand, followed me recently when we were speaking to women in the Treasury at 11 Downing Street, and when I finished asked me, 'How can you just get up and talk like that?' But the secret is that it's just practice really, like anything else.

What most companies want, when they invite a speaker, is somebody who can bring a different perspective. For example,

Barclays were trying to encourage more women to be really ambitious and get on the board, so I went to give them a bit of motivation, because it's something I am passionate about, that I can communicate in an honest and interesting way. I told them all a bit about my story, a bit about what I think of working in a male-dominated environment, how to juggle professional life and home life, and hopefully that was helpful. For me, giving talks is an opportunity to tell others what I have done, how I have done it, and to give them the encouragement that it is not all that complicated. I want to defeat this view that successful women are a special breed – actually you just have to work bloody hard, to have an idea, go for it and be dedicated to it.

And I write – not just this book, but my football column in the *Sun*, which I have written for seven years now. It's very gossipy, because gossip is what people are interested in, and it's fun. But I never identify my friends, so I don't get too much grief. Although I do get some! I remember Everton's chairman Bill Kenwright saying to me, 'I would love to write a column like yours, but I don't have the balls to say what is going on.' I just accept that not everyone likes it and see that as part of life. I also write a column for *Woman & Home* magazine, which is about my life and making it all work. I do enjoy writing but I have to be in the zone – I can't force myself. If I am up against it, I'll find I've got nothing to say. But it always comes in the end, and it's natural.

So at this point in my career I am enjoying doing a wide variety of different things. There are days when I can be in a meeting with Philip, followed by one with Lord Sugar, then off to see a government minister and then my football manager. They say variety is the spice of life, and I agree. And I'd add that nothing is work unless you'd rather be doing something else, and there's nothing else I'd rather be doing.

It does mean I have to be able to switch constantly between projects. In a single morning I can go from talking about high-street rents, to meeting the Government, to talking about the Olympic Stadium, to delivering a speech in front of 3,000 councillors as part of my speaking business, then to getting involved in sponsorship and season-ticket prices, and all the business and issues of West Ham. Luckily, I enjoy moving rapidly from one thing to another and have the ability to compartmentalise in my mind.

Still, while I have broad shoulders, some days it is pretty full on. As I write this, we are dealing with the re-tender of the Olympic Stadium, so I am being sent documents from our lawyers with a note saying, 'Can I have your comments back in an hour?' Then something happens at West Ham, Sir Philip Green needs something sorted out, someone from *The Apprentice* wants me to do an interview, *Woman & Home* are chasing me for a deadline, my son has got into trouble at school, and sometimes I just think, Oh shit.

It's 250 emails a day and a stack of paperwork and you just think, I don't know if I am coming or going. The only way to deal with that is just to accept that it has to be done. There is no way around it: you have to do it. I was jet-lagged, so I was up at three a.m., and even though I was exhausted by eight p.m. I had to work through until one a.m. the next day to get the work done. There is nothing else you can do.

I can envisage a time when I devote much more of my time to projects that are not about profit. I already do work for various charities, including the Stroke Association, the Mothercare Group Foundation, Wellbeing of Women, WellChild and Teenage Cancer Trust. And I get asked by other charities all the time, but you can only be effective if you limit yourself to a few.

Teenage Cancer Trust, to talk about just one, is the most wonderful charity. If you are a teenager and have cancer, you are either sent to the children's ward or the adult ward, and either way there is nothing for you to do. Your friends don't want to come and see you and sit in that sort of environment, so Teenage Cancer Trust raises money to create special teenage wards that have an Xbox console, Wi-Fi, pool tables, chill-out rooms and places where you can make your own food. They have take-out nights, DVD nights, and you can see the friends start to come and visit these teenagers, and it makes all the difference. It's an understatement to say that if you're 16-year-old boy surrounded by dying 80-year-old men, it is not much fun, and won't help your recovery.

That's why I helped head up a campaign to raise £1 million to build a teenage ward in Birmingham Children's Hospital. It was a wonderful campaign that I was privileged to be involved in, and the outcome has changed the lives of many young people who have been affected by cancer, in terms of their care, mental wellbeing and simply improving their environment.

I suppose, when you are young, you think you are invincible – that no one gets ill, least of all yourself – but once you have been touched by illness, as I have, once you have a bit more time to think about things, you become more giving. You've seen more of the world around you, and the best response to that is just to do something. When you see a 13-year-old who has had their leg amputated, who is six stone, whose parents need to be there every day but they have to spend £20 a time to park in the NHS car park to visit their sick child – you could end up hating the world if you thought about it too much. So you just have to think practically, what can I do to help?

That's partly why politics interests me. I wouldn't want to be an MP – I haven't got the patience for it all – but a role as some sort of government advisor or consultant would be very appealing. When David Cameron stood for Prime Minister, I was at a talk he gave where he said that he wanted to create an environment where business and the government were far closer, because that was the right thing to do. After all, it is business, not government, which creates jobs and wealth and tax revenue.

But I don't think that has been achieved yet. I think if you are a businessperson who employs people and you earn a decent salary, you are vilified for it. Instead of being respected because you give 50 per cent of your income to the taxman, there is no appreciation for what you are creating. The problem is that what has happened with the banks – and their bail-outs – has affected people's thinking about all businesspeople. Banks are businesses, so all businesspeople are bad is the (flawed) logic. Yet if you think about somebody who sets up a little enterprise employing one person and then two people, growing step by step – that is what business is really all about. Not the Bob Diamonds of this world and their multimillion-pound banking bonuses.

So I think it is really important to create respect for business and entrepreneurs among a new generation. It is crucial that we create an environment in which budding businesspeople can thrive. I still don't think enough is being done to champion small and medium-sized businesses, or to really argue on their behalf and articulate what it is that they need to be successful.

Setting up a small business can work really well for women who are looking to combine a career with a family, and there has never been a better time to do it, in terms of the grants that you can receive, the tax breaks, the assistance you can get. But you try finding that information. It is all in little bits and pieces scattered all over the place. There should be one place where you can go and say, 'I am starting up a business, I have £2,000 to invest' – a website with a matrix like GoCompare, where you can find out, OK, you can get office equipment for £500 here, you can get a suit for £200 there. There is a real need for tangible, independent advice that is easy to access, and that is something I would really like to be involved with: helping small and medium-sized businesses in some sort of official capacity.

And then it is back to what I outlined at the start of this book – my desire to help a new generation of young women come through. I want to help carve out an easier path for my daughter, Sophia, and her daughter, and all our daughters. So that these young women see no barriers in terms of the livelihood they want for themselves, and so that it is easier for them to combine earning a living with having a family. That's what I plan to devote my time and energy to in the future.

So, I come back to what I said at the beginning of this book, my call to arms, so to speak. I want women to know the truth: that with energy, determination and hard work you can achieve. You can build a career, a life, that both challenges and rewards you. That exhilarates and fulfils you. And I hope my story has offered you an insight into how I built a life that I love, and that I have laid out the building blocks to help you reach for whatever your goals, the life you want, may be. Have confidence. Walk tall. Be direct. Never be afraid to be a woman. The list goes on. And at the root of it all, have faith – in yourself.

I haven't tried to hide the cost of it all. The late nights, the phone calls, the juggling of work and family, the flak you might face along the way. The attention you will most definitely receive if you make a name for yourself in any world that has been traditionally male. But I hope I've communicated the highs, as well as the lows. The thrill of sealing a deal, the cut and thrust of business, the excitement of working with great people, learning and improving, all the time. The sense of camaraderie you have with your team, the colleagues who become trusted friends, the pride you feel when a business starts to turn around, when an employee starts to shine – when you have been behind that. The sheer joy of a doing what you love.

And the highs have more than outweighed the lows. In so far as it is possible – and you know what I think about that! – I have had it all. Work *and* family, refusing to make a false choice.

No, it won't be easy, but it will be worth it. I promise you.

CH.13
MY RULES
FOR SUCCESS

Over my working life, I have learnt that certain skills, habits and attributes are essential to achieving success. You will not instantly master them all. It will take time and practice. But if you follow these ten rules — and, importantly, *keep* trying to follow them — you will get very far along the road to where you want to go.

That I can promise you.

RULE ONE: WORK HARD

Success is about the relentless pursuit of what you want. Before you even start trying to get what you want, you need to accept that hard work is going to be a vital ingredient. It sounds simple, but a lot of people don't want to recognise that, because it's hard and it's work. I've known many people who really just want a get-rich-quick scheme, a shortcut to success. They are always chasing that one big deal. They don't realise that the path to success starts with the understanding that you will require dedication to what you want to achieve through hard work. You will sacrifice your 'spare time', you won't have a hobby and probably not much of a social life. But as you take the steps needed towards being a success, you have to remember that the first step is always hard work, and lots of it.

I work relentlessly to achieve a business goal, and I believe that is the single most important reason why I am successful. It may be two a.m. and I may be exhausted, but I keep working until it is finished. Whenever you are facing a huge pile of work or a major challenge, it is psychologically essential to have that acceptance. No matter how bad things are, no matter how hard the battle you face, you have to accept the reality of the situation, and embrace the pressure. You just have to take the view that it has to be done. This takes self-discipline and energy, and you'll not meet anyone successful who doesn't have both.

In my case, I think my energy is partly a compensation mechanism for the things I don't have. I don't have every quality that you need to be a really successful leader – I have one or two. I've met people who have them all, but they are exceptional. Most people are like me, in that you can compensate for areas where you might not be as strong.

The Olympic Stadium – if we get it – will be, for me, the ultimate example of a success that was down to hard work. Down to gritting your teeth, relentless energy and hard work. We have faced hurdle after hurdle with that project, but my attitude is that they're there to be jumped over. We'll do our best and we'll wait and see. And if we do get it, the great thing is that it is something that we really know is worth having.

But, in order to push yourself, to have the discipline to work that hard, you do have to really want it. If I was asked to run a marathon, I'd probably drop out halfway through because I've got no desire to do it, it's not on my radar as something that is important to me. Whereas if you find something that you love doing and feel passionately about, it won't feel like hard work. If you don't, you will never summon up the energy when you need to. You will be beaten pretty quickly because you don't care about it enough. Remember that nothing is work unless you'd rather be doing something else. So pick a career where you won't want to do anything else.

Very often it's that 'care about' factor that underpins everything in your life, be it your reputation, your business, or your employer. If you don't care about them, then everything is a struggle, and there will be only so much you can force yourself to do.

And I do believe that, if you want to succeed, the work never stops. I find the idea that you would *want* to turn your mobile or BlackBerry off, for example, completely strange. You read about people keeping their BlackBerrys by their beds, as though it were some sort of crime. I disagree. And it's not about being prepared to be available – it is about *wanting* to be available. I know, given the staff I have now at West Ham, that if I said at three o'clock in the morning, 'Right, we've all got to get together,' they'd come. That's the sort of enthusiasm I am looking for. I have it myself and I don't employ anyone without it.

There are of course times when I really, really don't want to do things, but somehow I find it within myself to do them. I think that comes partly from being at boarding school from an early age, from having to tolerate that lifestyle, and partly from an innate ability just to grit my teeth and do it. But it's like a muscle, in that you can develop that ability: the more you steel your resolve and make yourself see something through, the easier you will find it to do so the next time.

It would be unthinkable to me not to work hard, whatever job I found myself in; it is ingrained in the fibre of my being that what you get out is tied to the effort you put in. And even if you are in a job you don't particularly enjoy, it is better to work hard. You will get more out of it, and you are more likely to be able to move on. Someone once said that if you worry about the job you're in, the next job will sort itself out – and I think that's very true. Remember: to be able to work hard and persistently is a quality that not a lot of people have. You stand out if you're prepared to do the stuff that's not much fun.

RULE TWO: HAVE CONFIDENCE

Confidence lies at the root of personality. I meet a lot of professional people who don't have any personality, and therein lies a problem. Whatever qualifications you have, personality is at least as important, because people do deals with people, not with brains. When it comes to choosing between two people who have the same qualifications, you choose the one who has the personality you want to work with.

Confidence expresses itself as energy, as being able to articulate your thoughts, having an opinion, being able to be a bit charming, and being a good listener. But you can have too much confidence. There is a fine line between enthusiasm and delusion. Success is about ability as well – there are lots of people who are very confident but they can't deliver. They soon get found out.

To lead a team, you need confidence. Some people who lack confidence are scared to take on a managerial role because they think they need to be able to do every aspect of the work. But what really sets you apart as a leader is not how much you know how to do, but how you behave when you don't know what to do. If you don't have the confidence to ask for advice or to gather people together or to listen to people, you will not succeed.

You also need to have the confidence to avoid the my-way-or-no-way mentality. The best leaders are not afraid to work with and listen to people across a broad spectrum, and they get excited when they meet people better than them. That's because they are confident in their own ability. I have met some leaders who have refused to hire people because they think they may be better than them and therefore might challenge them and put their own position at risk. These are my least favourite type of people. If you care about what you do, you want to employ the best, and that may well mean you employ people better than you. Full stop. And if you do employ some-one better than you, you ultimately prove you are better than them, because you have shown that leadership in taking them on.

I am confident, and it has helped me at many points in my career, but I know that lack of confidence can be an issue for a lot of women. So I think the best advice if you feel you don't have the confidence to do something is to ask yourself, what have I got to lose? I remember when my sister-in-law didn't get a place at the university she wanted to go to. I said, 'Why don't you turn up and talk to them and see if you can get it? What have you got to lose? You don't have the place anyway, so what difference would it make?' And she did go, and they did give her a place. Who dares wins! And practice builds confidence. The more you put yourself out there, the more confident you become. The more you take a risk and approach someone, the easier it will be.

There are also little tricks you can use to boost confidence. Some people get really nervous at the thought of going to a networking evening, because they don't know anyone. First of all, I'd say that if you are going to give up your time to go, make sure it's worth your while. That will cut out quite a lot of needless worrying! And, if it is worthwhile, work out in advance who you want to meet and why, and think through what you want to say to them. It doesn't have to be Shakespeare. 'I came along tonight because I really wanted to meet you' is always a great opener! Then always follow it up with an email: 'I really enjoyed meeting you last night, I enjoyed discussing this with you and thought you might be interested in that.'

Think about what image you want to leave with people. When I started work, I wanted to leave the image that I was a professional, polite person, who was engaging and intelligent, and these things build up into one personality as you get older.

RULE THREE: EMBRACE AMBITION

'Ambition' can be a bit of a dirty word. People think there's a very fine line between being ambitious and being ruthless. I don't. I think if you're ambitious you have to embrace that; don't be afraid of it. Most successful people like a challenge, and that's what they thrive on – the next challenge. Ambition is simply the spark, that inner pride, that drives you on to be a success, and to keep being a success. We all know who the ambitious people are in our organisation. They set themselves apart. They understand that, if they don't champion their career, who will?

Competitiveness is part of ambition, and represents another area that can be a problem for some women. They think, If I'm competitive, that means I'm ruthless, that I'll walk on people and I'll do anything. But, actually, being competitive is a great talent – it is about the ability to push yourself because you want to be a winner, it's about having that inner strength, that little spark, that occasionally goes off and makes you think, No, I'm going to win. Women have to tell themselves that there is nothing wrong with that. Embrace your competitiveness!

Of course, not everyone wants to be chief executive of a big conglomerate. Most women want to have a job that suits them, that respects them and pays them well, and that is an ambition in itself. It is about working out what you want and then having the confidence to go for it.

A lot of people say to me, 'I hate my job,' but they don't do anything about it. So I think using your ambition is about deciding what it is you really want to do, committing to it, and then working out how, realistically, you can get there.

Road-map it. If you are in a job and you want to do better in that job, how are you going to get ahead? How are you going to get noticed? How are you going to take on more work? How are you going to show that you are more capable than perhaps you have already shown?

Make yourself visible and heard. Women can be shy of approaching their boss with ideas, because they may lack confidence. But good bosses love nothing more than people saying, 'I have got this great idea and I know how to implement it and this is the effect it will have on the company. It will make us more efficient, it will make us more profitable, it will make us better.'

It is all about taking that first step. If you're in your office and you think you do a pretty good job, what are you going to do about it? Work out what you want. Do you want a promotion? Do you want a pay rise? Do you want flexible working? These things don't often come to you – you've got to be ambitious enough to recognise you want them and then work out the strategy for getting them. Bosses are often seen as unapproachable, almost mystical figures who lurk in the background. But we often want somebody to walk into our office and say, 'I thought I'd bring to your attention that in the past I've done this, this and this.'

Plan how you are going to make your approach. Write down what you want to say, in short sharp bullet points and then, if possible, try to meet the person face to face. Just say, 'Look, I know the company has got an issue with this, I have come up with a solution that I think will work for the company, how would you prefer me to let you know? I can do it face to face in 10 minutes or I can write you a report. Which would you prefer?'

Some women curb their ambition and hold themselves back because they are concerned about how they going to manage it all. God forbid that you wave a magic wand and get what you want – how do you then manage everything else? Home, children, family? My attitude is to say yes until you say no. Go for it and then find a way to manage it. Or go for it and then negotiate a way to do it that will make it manageable for you.

RULE FOUR: HAVE THE COURAGE TO TAKE A RISK

Courage is crucial if you are going to get anything off the ground. You have to take some risks and you need to be able to make some tough decisions. I think I am naturally brave – it's that what's-the-worst-that-can-happen attitude – but courage is absolutely something you can cultivate too. You achieve some success, so you realise you can make good decisions, and so you take another decision, and another one. And your courage to take those risks grows.

If the prospect scares you, remember that you can start small. Nobody ever started anything without taking a risk, it's true, but it doesn't have to mean re-mortgaging your house and putting everything on black or red – that is not the sort of risk I recommend. Very often it is a risk with yourself and your time. When I first started out in business I was always the first person in and the last person to leave, to show that I had real enthusiasm for what I was doing, and I volunteered for everything. That was a risk I took – whether all that time, that graft, would be worth it. It was.

You will never know the outcome of anything unless you take the first step, and that is about risk-taking. It's like when I was asked to do *Comic Relief Does The Apprentice*: how could I have known that would lead on to me carrying out the interviews for the main show, which then led on to me becoming one of Alan Sugar's advisers?

Calculate the worst thing that can happen and be comfortable with it. If your life savings are at stake and you could lose everything, to me that would be a risk too far. But if it is that you hate your job but are too scared of rejection or the unknown to put yourself out there, you need to stop moaning and do something about it. Make a plan. Work out what you want to do, what will suit you and start networking and sending out your CV.

Don't be afraid of things going wrong. Things go wrong at work every day here at West Ham. My job is to deal with that, and it is about finding a way through. Before you achieve success you nearly always face temporary defeat – sometimes total failure – and the easiest thing in the world is to just walk away. And that is what most people do. Success is about having the backbone to work a way through.

In life there will be problems, that's a given. It's how many solutions you can find to solve your problems that directly equates to how happy a person is. West Ham has been a good example of that. The hurdles have been endless, and yet as I write this we are at top of the Championship, looking at promotion back to the Premier League. Very often the hardest fights are hard because they are really worth winning, and it is about having the will and the energy to carry on. This is something I believe in deeply. As with the Olympic Stadium, I certainly won't go down without putting up the very best fight I can.

It may not work out, and you also have to have the courage sometimes to accept defeat, and deal with it as elegantly as possible. Sometimes your best isn't good enough. Sometimes the outcome is not always in your control.

That's partly why I think the ability to move on is very important. Once I close the door, it is closed and I never look back. Things don't always go your way, but if you constantly carry that around you won't have the courage to try anything else. You will always be looking over your shoulder.

It is just as important to close the door on successes as well, or you may not have the courage to take on new challenges. I have known several football managers who won't take a job they consider risky because they have got this great reputation and they don't want to put it on the line. But why are you holding that reputation so close? If you don't believe in it, it is not sound, and there comes a point where it is holding you back.

I believe the things you regret in life are the things you don't do rather than the things you do. In that vein, if someone says something to you and you are burning to say something back but you don't, you will often regret that you held back. But – perhaps contrary to received wisdom – you rarely regret saying it, I find. To me it is about assessing risk. Weigh up not saying it as opposed to saying it: which is the most difficult?

I do stick my neck out and say what I think publicly from time to time, and I have been told more than once that I am too brave. I have no desire to cause trouble for myself but I do think that, if you believe something is right, you have to stand up and say so.

RULE FIVE: TAKE A REALITY CHECK

You don't have to be super-talented academically to be successful, and you don't need to be good at everything. But what you do need to do is work out what you are good at. Then you need to get better at it, and focus your career on it.

Everybody is good at something and most people, if they look into themselves, will know what that is. It might be that you are calm under pressure. It might be that you are a good organiser. It might be that you have great vision. It might be that you understand strategy. It might be that you are very good at figures. It might well be that you are good at figures but really bad at vision, and that's fine – we are not all Renaissance men (or women).

Give yourself a diagnostic test and isolate what you enjoy and, realistically, what you are good at. The second part is very important – I love art, but if you put a gun to my head I couldn't draw, so it would never have been a career that I could have pursued easily. You need to have realistic goals, as well as being realistic about your talents. I can't have an ambition to be a supermodel like Elle Macpherson, because it is never going to happen.

A lot of people love the idea of something. They love the idea of being a writer, or they love the idea of working on a magazine, but they can't write and they can't take photos and they are flogging a dead horse.

Instead, think about what you do well all the time and probably take for granted. Lots of women come to me and say, 'I have been stuck at home with the children for 10 years and I don't know what I am good at.' Well, you are organised, you can budget, you manage people well – we all have talents, and it is about working out what those are.

Be prepared to work your way up. People think that if they become a secretary that is it, but it can be the first step to doing other things. It is not the first job you get that matters; it is the last. You want to work in a certain company or a certain environment? Take the first job that is available and work your way up.

Then, when you reach the top, you need to be realistic about what is happening in your business. Lots of people who run big organisations don't want to look in the nooks and the crannies, because it is all so bloody difficult. Much easier to stick your head in the sand. But you need to find out what is going on. It is like peeling back the layers of an onion until you get right to the core – and then you understand. You can't change the culture of a company unless you do that.

There are always issues that arise in businesses that require confrontation, and lots of people avoid it because it is difficult and it takes a lot of energy. It is far nicer to be liked than not to be liked, but you can end up compromising your beliefs, your way of doing things. I think it comes down to integrity and professional responsibility. I am paid to be the person who says no, the person who pulls the plug on something, the person who says that, no matter how tempting, if it is not right it shouldn't be done. As the leader, you are the company's conscience, and it is very important to take that responsibility seriously.

RULE SIX: LEARN TO JUGGLE

If you have a family and a career you will need to learn about efficiency – and fast. You have to be able to get your work done and get out of the office, but you are competing against men whose hours can stretch into the evening. Organisation is the key to being as efficient as possible with your time. When I am in the office I work relentlessly. I don't surf the Internet, I don't waste time chatting, I do what needs to be done because I know that, when it is done, I can go home.

Deal with things as they come up. This is a habit I notice in many successful people, including Philip Green and Alan Sugar: when something comes up, they deal with it immediately. If someone emails me wanting an answer, it's much quicker to read it, answer it and move on to the next thing than park it, and then think, Oh, I've got to go back and do that.

Achieving a lot is about breaking things down. I'm a great one for systems, so I put all my emails into categories: one for urgent, and then others, for my various businesses. And then I take care of them in order of priority and just deal with them. There's nothing more satisfying than getting to the last one.

You do have to work out how to prioritise between your responsibilities. There are no hard and fast rules on this, because home is sometimes the priority and work is sometimes the priority. You have to have an acceptance that you can only do what you can do.

Remember: at work, the things that are important are the things that are either crucial to your business or to your career. You can't do everything. When it comes to the social side of work, at the end of the day, like many women, I would prefer to be at home. And it is OK to be picky about the invitations you accept. You have to ask yourself: why do I want to go, what do I want to get out of it and who is going to be there that I want to see? Or is it just that everyone is going to the pub and therefore I feel I should? Well, unfortunately, you can't, so you just have to say no.

You have to do the same as a parent. If you have a career, you can't be there all the time and you have to accept that and not beat yourself up. Listen to your children. They will let you know if they need more of you.

Accept that you can't do everything. Last night, I went home and my house was an absolute tip. I am the tidiest person I know and I thought, I'll have a bath and a lie down and then I'll get up and do it. So I had a bath and got into bed at half past seven and woke up at quarter to seven this morning! Sometimes you just have to give in.

Good childcare makes all the difference, in whatever form it takes. As I write this, we are under pressure at West Ham, plus I am in the middle of filming *The Apprentice*, and it's the summer holidays. But I am feeling relaxed because my children have gone away for a month with their grandparents, so I know that they're happy, active, entertained and safe. That is a huge, huge burden taken from me. I'll be flying out to spend a few days here and there with them as they tour around Italy.

RULE SEVEN: PLAN TO WIN

Fail to plan, and you plan to fail! My organisations are run with military precision. Nothing is left to chance, and that creates an environment of relentless energy. People know they have to deliver and they know exactly what they have to deliver. It is like a machine. The information goes in and everyone knows what they have to do with the information to achieve the right outcome. The culture is demanding but fair.

When a big problem arises it can be daunting, but if you look at it again you realise there is never just one big problem: it is always made up of lots of little issues. So, in the same way, I approach a huge task by breaking it down into small steps.

What's achievable? Where are you prepared to negotiate? Where can't you negotiate? What is your bottom line?

Break down the problem, work out the steps to the solution and resolve each one, step by step. You can use this approach in every area of your life, in fact. When I had my brain surgery, I broke it down into five steps: 1. Accept I had it. 2. Choose the procedure to deal with it. 3. Have the procedure. 4. Recover from the operation. 5. Get on with my life.

In the office, I like to get everything up on a board so that I can visualise things more easily, and draw out a work plan from that. We stick Post-it notes all over the board and then sort them into three groups: easy, more difficult, almost impossible. Then we work out what needs to be done, when it needs to be done and who is going to be responsible for it.

You can see on the board what the real crunch issues are – as well as what our bottom line on that point is, who we want to negotiate with on the other side, how we move the person that we think is the most reasonable from the opposite organisation. Then each one of those challenges becomes a project in its own right.

Pick the best person with the best skills for each task, and identify clearly who is responsible for which part of the task. For some managers it can become about glory hunting – the big pitch, the big delivery – and they want to do it all themselves, regardless of their personal strengths. But if you want to win you have to pick the best person to deliver what has to be done.

You need timelines. In football, for example, if you want to win the league, that means that by Christmas you have to be in the top five, and by Easter you have to be in the top two. You need deadlines, because otherwise you get constipation in the system. Nobody can make a decision, and there is a knock-on effect to everything else.

It is also essential to create a really good team spirit, so that people feel that winning collectively is important. It is really about communication. If everybody knows what their individual role is in the overall success of the task, and they know what everybody else is doing and understand that you win together as a team, then you create the best energy.

RULE EIGHT: KNOW HOW TO NEGOTIATE

I love doing deals. It is all about being resilient, relentless and persistent until you get where you want to go. But the interesting thing is that most people don't really know where they want to go. You need great strategists in business, not just great negotiators.

Negotiating is not about being tricky. The way I see it, when you are doing a deal you go in, you do the best you can to represent your company or yourself, you have a clean fight, and at the end of it you should be able to shake hands and walk away. Because you might win this time, but you won't win every time.

Having a reputation for being able to do good deals and fair deals is very valuable.

The first rule of negotiation is to know your bottom line. Work out what you can go to and stick to it. I work out what is commercially realistic and I am rigid about it. Accept that no one ever starts where they want to finish – everyone starts with enough room to compromise somewhere in the middle – so you have to know where you are prepared to compromise and what is your bottom line.

If you don't achieve your bottom line, be prepared to walk away. You will do your best deals when you have that mind-set, because the other person will recognise it, and will put more on the table. Often, you only get the pay rise you want when you have another job lined up, and that is because your approach is more confident. Your boss senses that you are prepared to walk away.

I am much more likely to walk away from a deal than many of my other colleagues, and I think that is because I don't mind saying no, and I don't mind a tough negotiation. It is when you become very emotionally attached to something that you tend to pay more than you should, or, if you are desperate to sell, that you take less than you should.

Good negotiation is also about persuasion. When we are doing a deal for a footballer, we might not be able to offer as much money as a richer club, so we have to offer other things. We have to be persuasive: this is the right club for you because these are our ethics and this is how it would suit you. If you go to Manchester United you might never play in the first team, whereas here you are coming straight into the first team.

Always remember there are alternatives. Never get into the mind-set that you need this player or this job. If you are looking for a new home, the key is not to fall in love with one place. Put offers on three or four houses and look at it as a commercial proposal. The worst possible mind-set to have in a negotiation is to think: 'I have to have that, I can't have anything other than that.' There is always another option.

RULE NINE: GRASP THE BOTTOM LINE

As an employee, you will really stand out if you have an understanding of your company's finances. Most people haven't got a clue. Sometimes people are aware of the income they generate, but they don't understand what it costs the company for them to generate that income. Have an eye for things that will save money and things that will make money, and you will stand out.

As a manager, you need to engage the staff with the financial side of the business and train them to think like entrepreneurs. Give them updates of where the company is, what contribution each department is making towards that, and the importance of always keeping an eye on costs.

In my businesses I always have a cost committee, where less senior people within the organisation watch what more senior people do in terms of expenditure, and that is very effective. The committee earns a bonus as a percentage of everything they save. It gives a real openness to the organisation and gets people thinking about the importance of saving money for the company, about making the company more profitable. The result is that you make a company better.

The best businesses, whatever their size, have a small-business mentality. People who work there know what things are cost-ing, they understand the difference small margins can make to the bottom line. My companies always have a proper purchase-order system, whereby everybody who wants to order anything has to detail why. Then they have to have three quotes attached to it. If they don't want to go with the cheapest quote, they have to explain why. These sorts of procedures keep everybody thinking about the bottom line.

RULE TEN: COMMUNICATE

I've said it before and I'll say it again: good leadership is all about communication. The people who work for me know exactly what is expected of them: they know what I think, they know where they are going, and they know what the rewards are going to be if they get where they need to go. And that's because I am very straight. People know where they stand with me, and that's essential. I can't stand people who say one thing and do another; there just aren't enough hours in the day to deal with it.

It is also really important to get your public message right, and very often you might need different messages for your staff, for your customers and for your shareholders. You need to find the best ways of communicating to all of those groups, so you make sure you have the best press officer, form the right relationships, whatever it is you need to do.

When things go wrong, remember that what people are looking for is a plan to put them right. You have to communicate that you can offer that. People want to know that you are doing everything you can to run the business in the most efficient manner, and they have got to have faith in your ability to do that. What they don't want to hear is your moaning. If there is a problem, they want to hear: 'I am the person that can resolve it, and this is how I am going to resolve it.' What they want, above all, is hope and belief in the people, the plan and the strategy.

In the same vein, if you run into a problem at work, the worst thing you can do is try to cover it up. You need to work out what has happened, what you think you should do, and be straight about it. Likewise, I believe that, as a manager, you should do your own dirty work. I hear stories of managers who have an issue with a member of staff and ask HR to have a word with them, but I think that is all wrong.

If you have to confront someone, deal with the facts, not the emotion. If you find somebody in your organisation doing something that you don't like, the first emotion is real anger, and that can make matters worse, not better. Don't let your message get clouded by your feelings. It is far more important to understand why the individual has done what they have done and what circumstances in the company allowed them to do it. How was the system breached? And then decide what you want the outcome to be. Do you want the employee to stay or to go? And then you have to put that into motion.

Very often, if someone works in an organisation they like for a person they enjoy working for, simply saying to that person, 'I am so disappointed in you,' is enough to crush that person. You don't need to get angry. Very often, simple things are dealt with in a very macho way. I prefer to do things in a slightly different way, to communicate that I think they could do – could *be* – better.

Ultimately, a lot of managing people boils down to managing what they expect of you, and you do that through communication. In that respect, it is very much like having kids: you have got to set ground rules! But unlike with your family, you have to be prepared to say, 'I am afraid you are not delivering and it is time for you to go.'

A FINAL THOUGHT

Perhaps my rules have inspired you. But perhaps you feel that getting started or getting further along your path to success is still daunting. So I want to strip things down to the basics a little further. Success means different things to different people, and everyone has a different measure of success. But whatever success means to you, there are always three cornerstones to achieving it. Planning, process and strategy.

Planning

Ask yourself high-quality questions. What is it you actually want? What is it you want to achieve? Then think about what has stopped you in the past. Why didn't I? What stopped me? Why didn't I achieve it? Decide what you want, decide what you're willing to exchange for it, set your goals and go to work.

Process

Just because you want it doesn't mean you're going to get it. Ask yourself what you have to do to achieve your goals? Plan your route to achievement. Set yourself the deadline and the targets. Be specific. 'Today I will write a fantastic CV. By Friday I will go and see HR and get a list of all the jobs available. By Monday I will have written my business plan and will take it to the bank manager.' This is the process involved in getting what you want. If you can't put yourself and your career first, then who will? Remember, worries are usual when thinking about change, but most of the things that you're fearful of never even happen.

Strategy

This is about the way in which you are going deliver success, by building on your strengths and resolving your weaknesses. It's the rules and guidelines by which you are going to achieve, the foundation upon which you build your planning and your process. You cannot deliver a strategy without having tactics – the actions you take to deliver your goal. And you will have to come up with a strategy specific to your circumstances, and be prepared to tweak and shape it as events unfold.

Finally, let me leave you with the motto that I live by, words from Calvin Coolidge, the former US president:

> Nothing in this world can take the place of persistence. Talent will not; nothing is more common than unsuccessful people with talent. Genius will not; unrewarded genius is almost a proverb. Education will not; the world is full of educated derelicts. Persistence and determination alone are omnipotent. The slogan 'press on' has solved and always will solve the problems of the human race.

And that's what I'll tell myself and say to you.

Press on.